VOLUM

UNCOVER YOUR

••••••••••••

EMPOWERING STORIES OF HOPE AND RESILIENCE

GOLDEN BRICK ROAD
PUBLISHING HOUSE

2022 Golden Brick Road Publishing House Inc. Trade Paperback Edition

Published in Canada for Global Distribution by Golden Brick Road Publishing House Inc. Printed in North America.

Paperback ISBN: 9781989819357 | ebook ISBN: 9781989819364

Media: hello@gbrph.ca
Book orders: orders@gbrph.ca

Table of Contents

Introduction

"We are called to be a light for others. This much I know to be true. But first, we must find our own radiance and let it shine from within."
-Unknown

As I contemplate these words and how they've shaped my recent journey, I'm awe-struck by the number of factors that have come together to make this book a reality. The word "serendipity" comes to mind. And when these kinds of happy accidents occur several times over, you tend to sit up and take notice.

We've likely all experienced moments like this one when things happen seemingly by chance or coincidence. On deeper reflection, there's nothing accidental about them. These occurrences are by design and invite us to pause and soak in the wonders of life. You've heard the saying, "When the student is ready, the teacher appears." Well, I didn't realize it, but I was about to get schooled!

Rewind to the Fall of 2020 . . . my first co-authored book, *Women, Let's Rise*, had recently launched, and what a whirlwind of excitement it entailed! I'm forever grateful for the opportunity to be a spoke in that wheel. Special thanks to my dear friend Lola Tsai Small who introduced me to the project. The entire writing journey was a trial by fire in the best ways possible. I learned to listen within for guidance, trust the process before knowing the how-to's, and tap into an inner strength I had previously underestimated. All skills and outlooks that would serve me well in the months to come.

Another key learning moment for me was the experience of writing as a form of healing—one in which we can find strength in vulnerability. I had re-discovered an outlet that not only worked for self-expression but was also a gateway to a deeper level of self-awareness and empowerment. And I was hooked!

Now here's where things get interesting: a little seed had been planted during my first authorship project, and I wondered if maybe

I could initiate a similar experience for women, with a concept that I would develop and nurture to fruition. I can't say that it was a burning desire that I set out to pursue with great determination. At least, not at the outset. Rather, it was a gentle ebb and flow of ideas, visualizations, and, eventually, clear-as-day downloads from God/Spirit/Universal Source. Every single concept that surfaced during that time was centered on the light or source of energy that comes from within. But how do we shine our lights brightly when we've lost touch with who we are? It was this point of inquiry that resonated deeply and kept calling me back for further reflection. And that's how *Uncover Your Light: Empowering Stories of Hope and Resilience* was born.

"If you build it, they will come," the famously misquoted line from the 1989 movie *Field of Dreams* is so appropriate to describe what happened next. It's one thing to feel in your bones that your idea is worthwhile, but it's another thing altogether to put it to the test with real, live people . . . other than your mom! Fast forward to March 2021 and, after getting the green light from our publisher, I set out to find twenty willing souls to join me on this writing adventure. Yeah, no pressure! But here's what I found: The more I spoke about uncovering my light, the more I heard things like, "Aha" and "Me too" from the diverse group of women I encountered. Not to mention the connections that would literally fall into my lap, as if a magnetic force was moving this project forward on waves of momentum. This happened so frequently that a second volume of *Uncover Your Light* was conceived in June of 2021 and you'll have the pleasure of delving into its pages shortly!

I share this progression of events, not to pat myself on the back—although we, as women, need to do more of that, unapologetically—but to affirm what I regard as truth in recent years: when we say a brave "yes" to opportunity, the Universe has our backs and things will unfold in a myriad of unexpected ways. It's pretty remarkable, just wait and see.

My deep gratitude goes out to the talented, heart-centered, courageous women I had the honor of working alongside to create our compilation, *Uncover Your Light Volume Two*. These stories of hope and strength are about being the best version of yourself, which is a profound act of self-love. The nineteen co-authors who share their stories have faced their fears when the path ahead seemed dark and unknown, and they want to provide a roadmap for others who are on similar journeys. They offer insights from lived experiences that can serve as a survival guide for women from all walks of life.

Our co-authors live across Canada and the U.S., but they represent a greater spectrum of diversity than their current geographical locations would reveal. The array of various backgrounds and cultures has created a rich tapestry of experiences that come through in their writings. Their professions also cover a wide range—including first responders, health and wellness, life coaching, spiritual healing, education, entrepreneurship, and more.

The topics within these chapters are widely relatable, yet deeply personal. They address issues such as family breakdown and rebuilding life from scratch; personal trauma and upheaval; journeys of self-discovery and finding your inner strength; discovering your worth and living with purpose; the list goes on. You, our Dear Reader, will walk away with fresh insights, life lessons, and a multitude of practical tips that you can implement in your daily life.

What does it mean to uncover *your* light? How would that unfold in *your* personal situation?

What would the process look and *feel* like? For each of us, the answers will be vastly different. But the ways in which we approach life's challenges, and the tools we use to overcome them, are intertwined with common threads. Through these words, our intention is to give you a framework to begin to unravel any complexities that may exist in your life. When we shine our lights brightly, we become beacons of hope radiating throughout the world, and we unconsciously give others permission to do the same.

Each of us has a voice and message that matters, and bringing them to light will create ripple effects that will last beyond the life span of this book. This is how we can change both our inner landscapes and the outer world—by witnessing our truths, one story at a time.

Many of the courageous women whose stories unfold in these pages have encountered life transitions and the emotional trauma that often comes with them. In some cases, they experienced a gradual detachment and wandering from self, after putting everyone else first and taking whatever breadcrumbs were left over. Does any of this sound familiar? In every case, the authors tapped into an inner wellspring of hope and resilience, allowing their unique beings to be unearthed and illuminated.

I'm extremely proud of what each co-author has brought to this project because these words reflect their authentic selves, no holds barred or window dressing needed. And I'm super excited for you, our Dear Reader, to delve into these chapters and see which parts resonate the most. I invite you to activate all of your senses as you read, imagining yourself on the journey beside each woman. You may be surprised by the number of times you find yourself nodding your head in agreement, or yelling out, "Heck yeah!" in solidarity. We welcome these affirmations because they're signs of a knowing sisterhood and shared understanding.

As I read through these poignant stories over the months of our writing project, I was reminded of something I wrote years ago in *Women, Let's Rise*. Talk about foreshadowing!

"In this life, we get to own what we know to be true. We need to struggle at times and face adversity head-on in order to build resilience, but we don't have to face these moments alone: we can turn to others for support and guidance."

We are humbled and honored that you have chosen to turn to this book for a dose of support and guidance. Our sincere wish is that you'll find an abundance of inspiration for the journey.

Introduction by Lisa Pinnock

Chapter 1

Showing Up Female

Andrea Beneteau

"It is possible to show up in your power even when doubt creeps in and few people believe in you!"

Born into a family of three girls, Andrea was not raised to believe in gender-specific roles. She was raised with the understanding everyone deserves a fair shake. When the opportunity arose, she believed she could be the first female hired into the fire department. Unfortunately, not many shared her belief. She worked her way through plenty of muck and resistance with little support. She had to wear uniforms made for men, use washrooms shared by men, and still got knocked down for being a woman even though she earned her badge like everyone else. Although it was hard having to prove herself to the men around her, she knew her presence would change people's minds about what is possible!

"Being a pioneer is never easy." Learning from a young age she wasn't always welcome, Andrea had to fight to do what she loved. In doing so, she learned it was critically important, even her purpose, to show up as herself. As a woman.

Since retirement, Andrea loves to travel but spends her most precious moments with her little loves—her niece and three nephews. She was born, raised, and still resides in the Toronto area.

ig: dviousone911 ~ fb: andrea.beneteau

li: Andrea Beneteau

Into the Fire

The intense heat pushed me down onto my belly, like an infant lying helpless and immobile. The floor was already spongy and barely supported our weight. Thick smoke and darkness defied the daylight outside. The fire hose dragged through my hands—a welcome reminder I wasn't alone. All I could hear was my breathing, my heart pounding, and the crackling of everything around me burning. I crawled along the floor, sounding it for holes and feeling for bodies—not a second to consider my own mortality. Although we had no idea about the layout of the house or where the fire was burning, we moved swiftly through the smoke as though we had a calculated plan of attack. We needed to find the fire and hit it quickly before things got worse.

As I moved deeper into the structure, I counted doorways to help me remember my way out. Without the use of sight, my other senses were in overdrive. The further I advanced into the home, the hotter it was. I heard a window explode on my right—a signal that the hot gases were too much for glass, which likely meant it was too hot for us as well. The temperature in the room immediately dropped hundreds of degrees, but it wasn't enough. On my radio, I called the crews outside to request more ventilation. The temperature continued to climb. I hollered out to my partner to pull out, and although my command sounded barely intelligible through my facemask and heavy breathing, I was relieved to feel the hose pulling in the opposite direction. As we retreated, I expected the heat to let up a little, but it didn't. As every second passed, I knew the beast was getting angrier. We had one chance to get it right. When it comes to fire, there are no rehearsals.

Firefighting Was Hard But Being Female Was Harder

Firefighting is hard—even scary at times. Fire itself is completely unpredictable. It can hide in places and surround us before we even have time to open the nozzle. We are exposed to carcinogenic gases and temperatures that could melt the helmets on our heads. We teeter off ladders and the edges of buildings carrying sixty pounds of gear on our bodies. And that's all before we even start the actual work. That actual work starts when someone calls 911—often the very worst moment of their lives. Some of our patients die, no matter how hard we try. We bear witness to complete loss and devastation. Occasionally, we are the last ones to hold someone's hand as they take their final breath. The career impacts you in a way that nobody can ever explain. Often, the idea of a "hero" feels impossible to live up to. Despite our training and efforts, the job is rarely glamorous. It hardly ever has a Hollywood-hero ending. But the most difficult part of firefighting for me wasn't the plane crashes, car accidents, or apartment fires. It wasn't the homicides or suicides, either. We had the training and support to deal with all of that. The hardest part for me was something I shouldn't have had to consider—being female.

My Mission: Change!

My journey into the fire service did not resemble that of most firefighters. A good majority would tell you they'd dreamed of being a firefighter since they were kids. That wasn't my story. The act of running into a burning building while everyone runs in the opposite direction still sounds a bit nuts to me. So, what was it? After five years as a paramedic, I felt the desire for a change. There were no women in the fire department where I grew up. It wasn't a complete surprise. The so-called "world of equal opportunity" seemed awfully lopsided most places I looked. Well, my interest was piqued. I wanted to prove, to both them and myself, that it was possible. Nothing was going to get in the way of me leveling the playing field of this very male-dominated world.

I was raised in a family of all girls. My parents fundamentally believed we could do anything we set our minds to and always encouraged us to challenge ourselves. Because of them, I thought if I worked hard and proved myself, I would earn my place. Outside of the walls of our equitable home, however, I quickly learned the rest of the world wasn't always so fair. Even as a child, I had a nose for injustice. I constantly questioned why girls and boys didn't have the same opportunities. Situations that others saw as *normal*, I viewed as unfair. When the neighborhood boys were playing street hockey, I fought for a spot on the "skins" team. Not necessarily because I was on a mission to prove something, but because I wanted to play. The fact I was discounted just because I had a vagina made me furious. It stoked a fire in my belly early on that stayed with me for life.

Being the First

I entered the fire department with confidence. I was no stranger to pushing up against the status quo. This job would be no different. No women yet? No problem. The lack of women in the fire service made me want it *so* much more. With my fundamental qualities, the values my parents instilled in me, and years of experience in the male-dominated world of paramedicine, I thought I had the right tools to take on the challenge.

Step one: I applied and I got in—first female in my department.

What an amazing accomplishment it is to be the first! You stand out. You're unique. A real "trailblazer." At least that's what people told me. Some even referred to me as a pioneer. I didn't feel worthy to be lumped into such a prestigious category, nor did I want to be. The glory of being the first wasn't what drove me. I just wanted to get hired and do the same job as every other firefighter. I wanted to show it was just as normal for a woman to be catching a hydrant as a man. I used to jump off the fire truck and hear people say, "Is that a fireman . . . woman?"

It was as though they had just spotted a *unicorn* dressed in bunker gear. No matter what I did or how many rungs up the ladder I climbed, it never seemed enough to earn my place as a qualified, professional firefighter.

Losing My Power

I didn't even get through training before I started recognizing my disillusionment. I worked so hard but it was never enough. I had to prove myself more than anyone else ever did. That wasn't just my first year as a rookie; it seemed there was a dark, smokey cloud over me that barely let up in the years that followed too.

I didn't let it show. It just made me work harder. The lack of support, approval, acceptance, and positive feedback over the years toyed with my power. I went from a confident woman who was armed and ready for a battle, to a lonely person filled with self-doubt. It was scary to think I couldn't rely on my colleagues, especially when this profession requires us to have each other's backs. I wasn't a part of the team—I was an unwelcome outsider. "Good morning, vessel for my sperm," one captain would greet me. The deputy fire chief once introduced me to twenty-five new recruits as "someone he was sleeping with." I somehow grew accustomed to a daily pat on my ass from one captain, and a kiss or hug from another.

When you're told enough times you don't belong somewhere, uncertainty creeps in like an insidious, smoldering fire. It chips away at your strength. I began seeing myself through their eyes. For the first time in my life, I questioned my capabilities, my choices, my judgment, everything. I lost trust in the people around me and stopped relying on my intuition and common sense. I was stuck. I started to lose my fight. In my quest to be accepted, to belong, to be just "one of the guys" doing our jobs, I realized I was giving my power away.

One morning, I looked at myself in the mirror. I stood there in my uniform and decided I wasn't proud of the woman standing in front of me anymore. Fuck that! I was tired of being unrecognizable to myself. I had had enough.

The Turnaround

I reminded myself why I took this challenge in the first place—to prove I had just as much a right to be there as the guy sitting next to me on the truck. My approach shifted. Instead of working my ass off to fit in, I turned my status as an outsider into my superpower. It didn't matter whether or not they wanted me there. I was going to be a successful firefighter and to do that I had to make being a firefighter safer for all women. I was no longer okay with wearing uniforms made for men, using men's washrooms, or all sleeping and changing in one dorm, sometimes with colleagues who felt sleeping naked was acceptable. I spoke up. I didn't wait for change—I demanded it. You can imagine how that went. My safety boots went missing. Someone erased my name and badge number from the official roster board in the station as if I no longer existed. Even after I asked him not to, my captain slept naked in the bed next to mine. Imagine how uncomfortable it was to see his dick in my face when the tones went off when we had to roll out of bed in the middle of the night. Every room I walked into immediately went silent. I got hate mail. The list goes on. But guess what? Things began to change. Nothing earth-shattering, but slowly the momentum started. Policies changed. New stations were designed to meet everyone's needs. Uniforms were overhauled. Sure, they were small things, but they were a start. Compared to the many big things that still needed to change, however, it never felt like enough. But I reminded myself of a quote from the poet Ovid: "Dripping water hollows out stone, not through force but through persistence." My best ally was my tenacity—I wouldn't let up.

It wasn't easy. I took a lot of punches. The trade-off I made for regaining my power was giving up the need to feel accepted. That was harder than I thought—in fact, I'm not sure I ever really let go completely. What human doesn't crave a sense of belonging? It was necessary, however, for me to reclaim my power and see myself through my own eyes again. Reacquainting with myself was the best thing I did for me and my career. I felt safe again with her by my side.

From Idealist to Realist

Despite my struggle, and against all odds, I managed to move up the ranks to become the first female fire captain in my department. I thought a promotion would finally convince my colleagues I was the real deal. Guess what? I was wrong about that, too. I was in charge of large-scale incidents of complete devastation and mass casualties. I was giving orders to fire crews arriving on scene, to paramedics, police officers, hydro and other utilities, the media, and the public, and I was still surrounded by certain colleagues who didn't respect my position, capability, or contribution. At some incidents, my crews ignored my direct orders. Even when I was the first captain on scene, and therefore the incident commander on the fireground, other captains would arrive and override my decisions.

When I consulted with my colleagues at a fire, I was told, "You want to be in charge? You figure it out!"

I realize, looking back, how simple I thought the fight would be: Girl applies. Girl gets hired. People realize she can do the job and has just as much right to be there. They accept her. She changes the perception of what is possible. The end! Turns out, I was so wrong. Although they forced me to adapt in many ways over the years, the world I entered needed to adapt to me more than I did to it. I just didn't realize how much and how hard it would be for so many. The deep-rooted desire to maintain the status quo was more fierce than any of the roaring fires I ever crawled into, but in hindsight, I realize my presence was just as intimidating. I represented change and, therefore, loss. Loss of how it was and how it would never be again.

Out of the Fire

It's hard to measure the impact my presence had, not only in the fire service but also in the community. Every time I showed up on a call, I hope I changed someone's mind about what opportunities are available to them, especially young girls. I know I helped carve out a path for the women who followed me, making it a little more "normal" for them to be there.

When I look through the lens of the people whose lives I touched, and in some cases saved, I believe my resilience, stubbornness, and tenacity helped keep my eye on the prize and prove what was possible. I made a difference in the community where I grew up. I made captain. I made myself and my family proud. There's no doubt I struggled with being the best version of myself throughout my career—not for lack of trying. Maintaining my power was a key piece to my survival. Through my own journey of self-discovery, I realized: one should never let other people's views distort the version one has of oneself. Easier said than done, of course. It took being retired, a lot of therapy, good friends, family, and plenty of wine, to understand how my sacrifice helped to move the inclusion pendulum just a little bit. With all the stories I could share about saving lives and property, with almost three decades of being a first responder, it seems the most important person who was saved and came out alive was me!

Chapter 2

The Opportunity of Betrayal

Stéphanie Rourke Jackson

"It's not what happens to you, it's how you handle it that shapes your life."

Stéphanie is a high-energy, coffee-drinking, naturally curious problem solver who likes to push limits. As founder of Beacon Coaching & Leadership, she is a coach and mentor for ambitious people who want to grow their confidence, crush limiting beliefs, and discover their full potential. She is the creator of the radical self-awareness program and life plan called Identity Mapping. Success stories, especially the ones where the protagonist overcomes adversity, inspire Stéphanie. She's known for her active listening skills, critical thinking, and ability to see new perspectives. Transparency is her superpower! Stéphanie doesn't take life too seriously; each day she seeks joy and laughter like medicine. Her husband of thirty years and her three children love to hang out together, share funny stories, and enjoy live music. You can often find her at the beach with a good book or running on a trail while listening to a motivational podcast. Stéphanie is a firm believer that nothing is impossible when you know who you are and have a solid support team!

beaconcoaching.ca

ig: beacon_coachingca ~ fb: Beacon Coaching & Leadership

li: Stephanie Rourke Jackson ~ t: beaconcoach

Thursday, August 25, 2011, was another beautiful, humid night in Toronto. Soft air, I call it. The youth group had just left my house and half-full bowls of chips still sat on the table. I poured a glass of wine and noticed there wasn't any milk for my cherished morning coffee. I glanced at the clock on the microwave: It was just before 11 p.m. and the local drugstore was open until midnight. Fantastic! I grabbed my keys and phone and headed for the door. I was pleasantly surprised to find my husband in the hall. He'd had band practice that evening and typically wouldn't get home until well past midnight. I greeted him with a smile and gently danced past him, suggesting he pour a glass of wine so we could have "date night" when I got back—all three of our kids were at an overnight camp that week. He mumbled something about being tired and asked if I really had to go out now?

"Hon, we have no milk for coffee in the morning. I'll be right back."

Off I went. I had no idea that in twenty minutes I would experience the crushing blow that would shape the rest of my life.

Until this point in our nineteen-year marriage—and truthfully, in my life—I had never met a challenge I couldn't handle. "Be strong" was a mantra woven into the cellular fabric of my familial being. I was the eldest of four children. We moved from Montreal to Toronto when I was six, during the "mass exodus" of the early '70s when the effects of the FLQ terrorist group caused fear and adversity. My parents were concerned for their young family, so we moved to the 'burbs of Toronto to live a comfortable middle-class life filled with family vacations to Barbados, multiple cars, and shopping sprees at Holt Renfrew. A pretty charmed life, actually.

From the outside, everything looked perfect. We appeared to be the ideal family, which was a cultural norm at the time. Yet, I sensed things weren't as they appeared. I was not brave enough to have the hard conversations about things like pornography, addictions, and cheating. Important conversations about true intimacy, healthy relationships, and transparency terrified me. Imagine if I had been that brave? I would have spared myself much unnecessary adversity. But, maybe, adversity is a beautiful teacher of resilience. It's almost impossible to become stronger without encountering hardship. I would get my chance to learn resilience soon enough.

"Don't air your dirty laundry where everyone can see it." Perhaps it was a cultural sign of the times or something I'd learned from my family, but that unspoken rule followed me as I grew up. Secrecy became my way of life. I feared if I didn't measure up to the expectations of others, I'd be rejected. I felt ashamed and wanted to hide my true self from everyone. The false front I put on taunted me, held me hostage, and slowly, I began to lose touch with who I really was.

At the same time, I had plenty to be grateful for: parents who truly loved us, enough food to eat, clothes to wear, the latest gadgets, dance lessons, and loads of friends. Even with the niceties of life, I regularly felt confused and lonely. A dark sense of not being enough—like something was missing. There was an ache in my heart, a craving for something more. I wanted to be known, to be heard, to be accepted for exactly who I was, flaws and all, yet I often felt like I was living outside of myself, looking back with my head cocked and my brows knitted together as if to say, "Just who do you think you are?"

I tried desperately to satisfy the yearning with anything I thought would give me that euphoric happiness that everyone else seemed capable of. I kept my secrets to myself and never shared my shadow side with anyone.

In fourth grade, I first felt the sting of rejection. Our class did a week of experiential learning at Pioneer Village. We dressed in 1800s attire and used the tools and learning style congruent with the period. I was asked to recite a math problem. Halfway through, I got stuck and couldn't produce the answer. My teacher encouraged me to start again. I could feel the heat develop in my gut, my throat tightened, and my brain froze. Again, I couldn't produce the answer. Using me as an example of what would have happened in pioneer times, my teacher told me to go sit in the corner. She put the dunce cap on my head and told me to face the class. My friends showed some compassion but most of the class just laughed which left me feeling stupid and betrayed. Like my shine had just been stolen from me. Later, I would come to understand this was indeed what shame felt like. If the ground could have opened and swallowed me, I would have gladly been consumed by it. Left abandoned and shattered, I wanted to run. Anger swelled up in me and in my brokenness, I vowed that no one would ever take advantage of me again. Protecting myself from getting hurt and feeling that unrelenting dread of embarrassment became my driving force. I learned how to cope by closing myself off to vulnerability and intimacy. I built big protective walls so I wouldn't get hurt. What doesn't kill you makes you stronger, right? The problem was, no one could get past the walls I'd built, not even me. This was the beginning of betraying myself.

I longed for deep, intimate, vulnerable, close relationships, yet I trained myself to be slightly aloof while also being just honest enough to push people away. Transparency and truth had always been strong values of mine. Somehow though, this made me a target for the label "bitch," a word I occasionally heard whispered in my vicinity. I was "too much" for some. My nonchalant attitude was "not enough" for others. All the while the real me was crying out to be loved, wanted, and desired. I made it my mission to try and attract men by flirting. This helped me fit in when what I really wanted was a sense of belonging. I made some bad choices, gave myself away too quickly, and then felt dirty and used when my heart was broken. I wrapped my identity around whether or not men liked me. My high-school years were consumed by this desire to be thought of as smart, bright, and shiny. Yet my inner critic taunted me: Who do you think you are? You're not interesting! Your sparkle has faded. Soon enough they'll leave and laugh at you!

I realize now that my self-esteem was flimsy; I had no idea who I really was and relied on external opinions to bolster me. I didn't have the internal tools to safely process my emotions. I angrily repeated the mantra of my familial youth: I am strong; I won't let them see me cry. So, I cried alone in the shower or while writing in my diary, tears soaking the pages, flooded with the emotions of my true self. I felt I couldn't share this with anyone. It was the '80s.

No one talked about their feelings; only weak people went to therapy, or so I thought. I remained locked up like my diary, exhausted from all the posturing I did most of my adolescence and adult life.

In my late teens, dating finally connected for me. The "boy next door" caught my eye. Rob and I began chatting on the street corner. A few casual dates lead to the brush of his hand at the park, then the softest yet most electric kiss I'd ever experienced. We became official and he bought me a promise ring. He was charming, kind, funny, creative, musical, and attentive. He had many friends, men and women. He liked to have fun, didn't take life too seriously, and did some radically risky things. We hit a couple of bumps early in our relationship; there were some red flags that I should have brought up but didn't. What if I was wrong? What if my truth scared him away? I did everything I could to not feel the pain of rejection. I didn't trust it would go well if I was honest. I chose to sweep that hard conversation under the rug and instead, I ran.

When I was twenty, I took off to Europe for a few months with a couple of friends—a beautiful escape from the external world that I felt kept rejecting me. Yet, the thing I couldn't get away from was myself. I flirted with other men, choices I eventually shared with my boyfriend. He struggled with what I told him and broke up with me. Trust: gone. Shattered. So many shower tears and diary entries describing what a terrible person I was. Why was I so stupid? I blamed myself for wrecking everything. The need to be desired was so compelling, it was actually destroying me. Even so, I didn't ask for help. I am strong; I won't let them see me cry. I added more layers to the fortress. After a brief break, we got back together but didn't deal with the pain that was still below the surface. We just swept it under the carpet and hoped it would go away.

After nine years of dating, although our carpet was getting quite lumpy, I presented Rob with an ultimatum: "Are we ever going to get married?" I shouted.

I couldn't stand the thought of attending another wedding that wasn't our own. "Um, yes?" he answered.

I took that as a proposal and the next morning we were at Ashley's registering for china. How ludicrous I feel when I think back to that time.What a crazy way to get started. We didn't tell anyone, not even our parents, about the engagement for three months. I figured, what's one more secret?

Our life after getting married seemed fine. A pretty charmed life, actually.

From the outside, everything looked perfect. We appeared to be the ideal family, and then something changed. There was a definite shift in Rob's behavior, although it came about in a slow drift. I felt that something weird was happening. I confronted him about some suspicions I had regarding his new work colleagues and the strange hours he was keeping. He looked me in the eye and told me nothing was going on. I had a choice to make: believe him and be a good wife, or be a combative, mistrusting nag. I chose to be the "good wife" but was tormented by my feelings of inadequacy, shame, and anger. I said nothing more. I buried it, as did he. We bought a new house and "moved on."

Until that fateful day twelve years later, on August 25, 2011, when I hit my rock bottom! Freshly home from the drugstore with a bottle of Tide in one hand and a carton of skim milk in the other, I considered which would be better to throttle him with as he confessed to the three-month affair he'd been having with a staff member at our church. Shocked and numb, I had absolutely no recovery tools for the anguish of this betrayal. All the posturing I'd perfected over the course of my life failed me. I was beyond lost. My identity—everything I thought I was—and my life as I knew it was gone. Who the f**k was I? Profanity spewed from my mouth as our framed wedding photos lay shattered on the ground–along with my heart.

After raging for what seemed like hours we were exhausted yet we did something incredibly normal: We folded the pile of clean laundry that sat in the middle of the bed. He went to sleep first, oddly relaxed for someone who'd just vomited out a deep, dark secret. I just lay there frozen, wearing the stench of the vomit while I bargained with God to turn back time. After what seemed like a sleepless eternity, I picked up my phone and looked up: "what to do after an affair?" My guts felt like they had been surgically removed without any anesthetic. It was pure hell. I couldn't believe that this was my life. That was when the first tears rolled down my cheeks.

I stood face-to-face with the impact of his incredible infidelity and had my first panic attack. This was disgraceful. What would people think of our perfect life? I needed help; we needed help.

Rob called our pastor, who graciously arrived at our house by 6:30 a.m. We hugged, poured coffee, and cried while mapping out a plan for our recovery. I will never forget our pastor's encouraging words to me. He said, "Stephanie, you have biblical grounds for divorce, but I really don't think this is God's plan for you."

I now had the opportunity to be part of his redemptive process. I clung to those words in the hardest months ahead, during our recovery and restoration. He also handed us a card for a counselor. Now I was going to be in therapy. Not just me, but us, and eventually our kids. It seemed so unfair. I remember the first meeting with our therapist, I screamed angrily at my husband, "For ninety-eight days of pleasure, you have now put me and others into years of therapy. How dare you!"

My new mantra became: I am not strong on my own, I will let them see me cry. We continued the hard work. And eventually, with counseling, recovery groups, personal coaching, spiritual direction, and the support of our friends and family, we gained strength. It didn't come from us. It came as a result of surrender and acceptance that we could not save ourselves. We dug deeper into our faith. Some days, that was the only way I could breathe. The pain was excruciating. Infidelity carries an enormously high cost. The journey is long and messy with many uphill battles. However, if you lean in, you can become more beautiful for having been broken. I learned the process of forgiveness so that I could let go of bitterness, contempt, and resentment.

My core fear of rejection had held me back from the intimacy I deeply desired. Through the opportunity of betrayal, I discovered the true me. My husband and I learned how to avoid sweeping the hard conversations under the carpet. I finally felt free! Some of the most precious moments in our restoration process were his heartfelt proposal on the beach in Florida on my birthday in May 2012 and a vow renewal celebration on our twentieth anniversary in October that year. My greatest adversity has now given me permission to become my greatest ministry.

As a healed, more compassionate woman, I now work as a professional life coach helping others to find their identity and the courage to live a life of deep fulfillment from a place of authenticity, transparency, grace, and confidence.

Recovery, resilience, and true intimacy are possible! It was just a heartbeat away, within me, not in posturing to impress others or the admiration of a man. It was my birthright. And now, I get to share the real me with my husband in our transformed marriage of almost thirty years!

Chapter 3

Out of the Wilderness and Into the Light

Denise Ledi

"We're all on a journey towards hope and personal fulfillment. It's even more meaningful when you're not going it alone."

Denise learned many valuable life lessons very young. Her mother died when she was eight. She quickly learned that one of the biggest myths in life is that we have all the time in the world. Also, when you have the right people around you, you can move through *anything*, soar to your greatest heights, reclaim and reignite your dreams.

Denise spent more than twenty years as a leader in addiction and mental health, forensic psychiatry, and corrections health before becoming an empowerment and executive leadership coach and consultant, public speaker, and writer.

Based in Edmonton, Alberta, Canada, and serving clients across North America, Denise couples real-world leadership experiences with her expertise as a certified executive coach. She is a Master's trained criminologist, which makes for an innovative, integrative, and unique perspective to help others achieve the measurable results they're looking for.

Wife, daughter, coach, and friend, Denise believes that we reach our highest potential by helping others reach theirs. Her primary mission is to empower others to become their best selves and access their full potential, and to make an extraordinary impact helping others shine their light on the world!

denledi.com

ig: deniseledi ~ fb: denledi

li: denise-ledi-coach

Realization

Okay, Denise: What is it? What's missing? What's wrong? What do you want?

January 1st, 2015. Another year heralded in at the stroke of midnight. I asked myself these questions as I watched the fireworks overhead in the cold night sky. I found no answers up there, only booming sounds and crackling pops, vibrant colors and shapes bursting upward into nothingness. Kind of like how I felt inside. Empty and void. I was stuck.

Maybe you know the feeling: a quiet dissatisfaction that you know is there, but you don't know why. To look at you, everything seems fine, but in reality, your soul is weeping, pouring out its discontent with a never-ending refrain inside your head. Mine went like this:

I'm so burned out. I don't know the difference between up and down. But here I go, stepping up to the plate and facing the day. Never-ending emails, people at my door, all competing for my attention. I'm beyond overloaded.

Oh well. I need to be present. Take it all on. Atta girl! Dig in. Keep driving forward. Get it done. No stopping. No rest. You can handle it: the dysfunction, the pressure, the stress. You're not some special snowflake.

Remember what you were told as a little girl? Give it your all, no matter what, or you'll never make it. People won't see you—much less recognize your abilities—if you don't. Until then, soldier on. I am drained, bone-weary, and tired, and I'm going to do it all over again tomorrow. Rinse and repeat.

My God. This isn't living; I merely exist.

That was me twenty-plus years into my career. I had climbed the ladder and gone from student to management. I navigated complex and challenging systems, chaos, and ever-changing environments.

I had the safety of a regular paycheck and the trappings of what some may define as success. The upper-middle-class lifestyle and all the opportunities that went along with it: career, home, marriage, and lifestyle. No kids, I'm "Aunty D" to all, by blood and by choice.

Don't get me wrong, I was and am beyond grateful for and very proud of everything I've achieved. It's an honor and privilege to play a part in positively impacting countless lives: clients and their families, staff and other colleagues, leaders, and friends. But I knew this: I wasn't put on this Earth to be miserable and burned out, grinding out a career spanning multiple decades. I envisioned myself as more than a great daughter, friend, leader, mentor, sibling, or wife.

I'm not here to travel through life and then . . . die.

I'm here for more. I believe we're all here to be, do, and have more—something meaningful and impactful.

To this day, I'm not sure what it was about January 1st, 2015 that changed me, if it was the spectacular images overhead, or perhaps the cold, or a combination of the two. But in those moments of wonder, my imagination piqued. I saw beauty amongst the stars in ways I hadn't in a very long time. The beauty of creation intersected with man-made design. Someone's dream was literally bursting forth with light, dazzling each and every one of us. In a sudden moment of awareness and clarity, I realized that whatever was amiss with me wasn't about work or the environment I was in. It was deeper. Somewhere along the way, I bought into stereotypical societal definitions of success, lock, stock, and barrel. I stopped dreaming and reaching for the stars.

I was living in my head instead of my heart, playing it safe instead of taking expansive steps forward. I was limiting my desires, natural gifts, and talents from reaching their full expression; I stayed hidden from myself and the world. Why? Self-doubt, fear of failure, and fear of judgment—my trifecta of limiting beliefs that unwittingly held me back from stepping into my potential and embracing life fully. I was living a life of missed opportunities and regret. And I had no one to blame but myself.

Have you ever experienced anything like this? Have you ever asked yourself, "How and when did I lose the essence of who I am?" I realized I had no clue how I got where I was, and even less of a clue how to move forward. This series of epiphanies, and a cry out to the heavens, was the beginning of the way back to me.

Discovery

Well, this isn't it.

Nope.

The first solution I came up with was to dive into leadership and personal growth books. I knew I had to show up differently in key areas of my life for change to occur. I attended conferences, participated in workshops, you name it. Anything I could think of to help me move forward. At times, a fleeting pinprick of light emerged. I was working *harder* than before, but the skills I learned gave way to old habits and results. Two steps forward, two steps back. It took another *two years* of this dance before I'd had enough.

Next up, I hired a coach. A leadership coach that specialized in performance and who happened to be a licensed clinical therapist. I needed someone to hold me accountable and help me work through and beyond the insights I had.

I am here to tell you that if I had known how much it would challenge me, stretch the limits of my comfort zone, and, at times, render me mute from sheer overwhelm . . . I'm not sure I would have done it. Yet, I'm so glad I did. I've *never* looked back.

Working with a coach changed me. I knew I had a lot to give, but I just didn't know how to get there. I had to get out of my own way and stop sabotaging myself. I had to peel back the inner layers of my life to become aware and understand my limiting beliefs. I had to transform fears rooted in stories created in childhood about how life works—stories and illusions I thought were real, but that prevented me from accessing the infinite possibilities of who Denise Ledi is.

My story begins with my mom and dad, new immigrants to Canada from Jamaica and Ghana, respectively, by way of the UK. They left behind friends and family to pursue their dreams. This was their chance, their opportunity to rise above and beyond 1960s societal beliefs, norms, and stereotypes to design the life they wanted.

I can still picture little Denise listening to and watching their hustle and grind; an engineer and nurse laying the groundwork for better days ahead for my brother, sister, and me. From observing my parents, I began to tell myself, *This is what it takes to be self-reliant. Success results from 'hard work and working hard(er). Can I achieve success too? What if I can't?* Little did I know that these formative beliefs, fears, identities, and reinforcing mantras were about to take on even more significance. Life as I knew it was about to take a catastrophic detour.

***

My mom got sick. Very sick. The doctors couldn't find what was wrong with her. It became common to come home from school and hear her being sick in the bathroom, then go in to find her covered in vomit, blood, and bile. My younger siblings, father, and I became less and less carefree and more and more responsible while the world continued. That's just how it was. I was becoming Little Miss Strong and Independent. My "strength" demonstrated that I could take on more and more, even when I couldn't. Helping out proved my worth. Taking care of others—and ensuring that I was one less thing for them to worry about—became my thing. I wore this identity like a badge of honor.

Over time, my mother became too weak to leave her room. Eventually, she went into the hospital. One day, she never came home again. She died. I was eight.

I saw her for the first time in months the day before she died. There she lay. I couldn't believe it. My mom: frail, gaunt, small. The seemingly invincible powerhouse was reduced to a shell. She called me over. My legs carried me towards her but I don't recall my feet hitting the ground. I grasped her hand; it was cold and weak. She tried to talk to me, but the only thing I could make out was my name . . . her voice was a whisper, a speck of what I knew . . . but I responded as if I understood her.

I believe that on some level, that wordless soul level, I knew what she was trying to say: "Don't be scared. Be good. You're going to be okay . . . you're going to be great and do great things, Denise! And of course, I love you."

For many years, remembering that scene brought sorrow and anguish. It was the end of hope and of life as I knew it. It was the end of truly believing in a loving, heavenly Father. My head warred with my heart mightily on this one. Having grown up in the church, attending Sunday school and masses, I believed that questioning my faith was wrong, that I was bad.

My formative years, my paradigms, my stories, my trauma: they shaped me. Invisible blocks and limiting beliefs became a form of autopilot for me, running my life as I began running amuck. I fed into societal- and self-constructs, as well as cultural and familial expectations. There was dissonance between who I was, what and who I wanted to be, and how I was perceived, personally and professionally. These beliefs were protective measures meant to keep me safe, but they kept me tethered to the notion that I didn't matter; my own needs and wants were prioritized behind family, friends, and work.

The Light

With the guidance of my coach, I discovered myself beneath the layers of false meanings and protections and embraced all facets of my life's journey. I identified, understood, and accepted my beliefs for what they were. True power is found within. Change is an inside-out job. It's not easy, but freedom comes from healing. As a wise friend once told me, "The wounds we hang on to show us where more love is needed."

In my case, this meant opening up, processing, and releasing stuck, unexpressed emotions and traumatic memories instead of remaining disconnected and disassociated from them.

I created a new truth about who I am and what I'm here to do. My meaning of "success" also changed. I recognized that success is in us and flowing all around us, and as Maya Angelou once said, "Success is liking yourself, liking what you do, and liking how you do it."

Today I sing a new song: a song of beauty, of ashes transformed into hope and strength.

The anger is gone . . . the sadness, the fear, the hurt, the guilt, and shame. Gone, gone, gone . . .

Because I am enough, I am good. I understand.

I can forgive. I forgive myself.

I'm free to express myself. I want to express myself. I have freedom.

I speak my truth. I live my truth. I stand in my truth, no matter what.

I'm seen. I'm heard. I'm healing. I'm releasing. I'm letting go and moving on.

I'm focusing on myself.

I'm certain. I'm complete.

I'm resilient and powerful.

I'm connected with myself and others. I'm connected with God.

I'm empowered by my emotions and I am continually growing.

I've embraced my purpose.

The dormant light within has sparked, and baby, I'm on fire! Lighting up the world, never to be diminished or extinguished again.

We all have our own unique way and version of awakening and of rising up to live our lives to their fullest expression. It's inspirational. It's powerful. It's what the world needs from every single one of us. This is why we're here.

Thank God we're always growing and evolving. Through awareness, acceptance, compassion, and forgiveness, we let go of old paradigms and create new meanings. As the great Jeff Brown said, "When we excavate our soul scriptures from their hiding places, we begin to walk in our own shoes. The path is not always easy, but we always know which way we are headed . . . you stop looking for it out there or up there. You find it right here, in the bones of your being. Breathing in, breathing out, here we are."1

This is my story: breakthroughs, challenges, insights, and everything in between. We all have a story. Perhaps you saw a bit of yourself in mine. Maybe you were encouraged and/or inspired. Maybe it sparked a memory that led to new insights about yourself. I don't know. But I do know this: sharing my authentic self,

1 Brown, Jeff. *Hearticulations*. Toronto, Canada: Enrealment Press, 2020.

having you bear witness to my life, sharing with you the things I wrestled with, may help you to discover and reclaim your brilliance and shine upon the world, simply by being you.

Believe. Believe in yourself. Embrace a new song.

Doing you is the way forward.

You can do it, Sister!

I know it. And I'm right there with you.

To your light!

Chapter 4

When Failure is Not an Option

Siobhan Carlin

"I believe that people come into our life for a reason, a season, or a lifetime, and it's important to be mindful of the lessons they are here to teach us. We may not always understand why things happen and unfold the way they do, but by living through many life lessons, I have learned that we need to have faith in the journey."

Siobhan Carlin has been a paramedic in Toronto for over thirty-one years. It's a career she never intended on having, but one that became a "calling" and has brought her much joy, sorrow, healing, and opportunity.

She is an avid traveler, a passion nurtured in her at a very young age, thanks to her father's *National Geographic* magazines. It was between these pages that she would disappear and spend hours exploring other lands. She made a personal goal to visit every continent and accomplished that by the time she was twenty-eight years old. The one thing that she always brings home from her travels is a resounding sense of gratitude and the realization that she is truly blessed to be a woman in this country with the opportunities and privileges that are available to her, something she tries never to take for granted.

She enjoys spending time with family and friends and loves nothing more than to host them in her home, where, so often, the best memories are made.

When she reflects on the life she is living today, it looks nothing like the one she envisioned for herself as a young adult. Although that took some time to accept, she simply tries to live in the moment and seize opportunities that come her way.

ig: siobhan.carpediem ~ fb: Siobhan Carlin

On a cold January night, my father died of a massive heart attack. I was sixteen years old. I remember telling my mom to go to the front door, turn on the lights, and wait for the ambulance. I stayed with my dad, cradled his head in my lap, and stroked his hair. To this day, I can still see the color of his face, the tightness of his jaw, and the tension in his neck. I kept telling him that help was on the way and that I needed him to breathe. What I didn't know at that time was that he was already gone and this would be the last time I would hold him and feel his warmth. He was never coming back. The incomprehension and helplessness I felt then are what eventually drove me towards my chosen career path and filled me with a desire to save someone else's father in a way that I was unable to do for my own.

That night is embedded in my heart. I remember the doctor came to tell my mom and me that they were unable to save him: "Your father is dead."

The information was delivered swiftly and with little emotion. I asked the doctor if I could see my father and I was ushered into a room that felt much cooler than where I had been waiting, everything in there was still and quiet. I noticed my father was on a metal gurney. His hair was completely disheveled, he had a tube coming out of his mouth, and his pajama top and bottoms were open, leaving him exposed and uncovered. Immediately, I set about "fixing him." I thought about how mortified he would have been if he knew how he looked at that moment. I gently combed over his hair with my fingers. I tied up his pajama pants and did up the buttons on his top. I looked at him one last time. It is that image I see when I close my eyes, to this very day.

From the time I was about three years old, I wanted to become a doctor. All of that changed when my father died. He was the sole breadwinner in our family and because my mother didn't work, I had to step up and take the lead. I worked three jobs while trying to finish high school. In those days, I often felt lost, like I was bobbing in the middle of a great big ocean, waves of emotion and responsibility crashing down on me, making me feel like I was drowning.

I became interested in the paramedic program when I found out it was a one-year college course. I enrolled in my high school co-op class and was placed with Toronto Ambulance, an opportunity that helped me get into the college of my choice. I remember the first co-op ride out I ever did. It has stayed with me, become a part of me, and, at the time, showed me that I had what it took to become a paramedic. I was eighteen years old. I had to drive to the southwest part of the city to start my shift at seven in the morning. I had no idea where this station was so I left my house at six o'clock in my faithful old car with my route planned, a map book in my lap, and ample time to get there. I arrived in plenty of time, so I sat in the parking lot listening to the stillness of the morning and watching as the sun started to rise over the city, wondering what the day might bring. I was riding out with two men I had never met before and, I'm not going to lie, I was nervous. Soon a pickup truck drove in. When the driver stepped out of his vehicle, I noticed immediately that he was tall, had a shaved head, was broad and muscular. In the next moment, another guy rolled in, riding a Harley Davidson. He wore a skull cap helmet and sported a handlebar mustache. His face was stern and he too was a solid-looking guy. I took a deep breath and managed to get out of the car and walk over to where they were. I introduced myself and, to my surprise, their faces broke into welcome smiles and we all walked into the station like we were old friends.

Our first call that morning was to an arena where a man had suffered a heart attack. Our update was that cardiopulmonary resuscitation, or CPR, was being performed by the police on the scene. We took off in the ambulance with the lights and sirens on; for a moment I couldn't believe the type of call we were driving to. We descended into chaos, the man in need of help had no heartbeat and he wasn't breathing. He looked the same age as my father had been when he passed, and we needed to get him to the hospital fast! Mr. Harley Davidson stayed in the back with the patient, a firefighter, and a police officer, while Mr. Pickup Truck drove and I sat beside him. We flew through the city with our lights and sirens on and I remember sitting quietly, my heart and mind racing, trying to take it all in. When we arrived at the hospital, I tried to stay out of the way yet be as helpful as I could. I opened doors ahead of the crew and somehow, instinctively, knew what was needed without being asked. We rushed this man into the Resus room where the team of doctors and nurses awaited our arrival. My crew told me I could stay in the room and watch what was going on. I stood in the corner quietly while the answers to all my questions unfolded in front of my eyes. I had always wondered what happened to my father the night they brought him in. I had wondered what they did and how it all played out that day. I watched it all in awe.

After some time, I was called out of the room to attend another emergency. This time we went to a construction site for a guy who partially amputated his leg with a saw. As it turned out, we took that patient back to the same hospital we had just left. Sadly, we found out that our previous patient had been pronounced dead. I stood against the wall of the emergency room looking out a set of glass doors and observed this man's wife and son being given the news that he was gone. I watched the wife crumble and the son (who would have been about my age) suddenly stand up straighter and protectively put his arm around his mother. At that exact moment, I witnessed a boy become a man. It was as if I was watching the replay of my own life two years prior. I could feel the familiar tightness in my chest, the heat of tears behind my eyes, and I knew I had to hold myself together; this was not the time or the place to fall apart.

I drove home that night in complete silence while thoughts from the day filled my head. I got home, closed the door to my room, and gave myself time to sit with the day. Finally, after two years of keeping it all in, I let the hot, wet tears fall freely and allowed space for the unbridled sobs of sadness and relief to follow. I finally knew what had happened the night my father was brought to the hospital. I cried for the boy today, who suddenly became the "man of the house," understanding all too well what his journey ahead looked like. I cried for the young girl who I still protected, somewhere in the depths of my heart; for the lessons she was forced to learn and the harsh realities that were thrust upon her all too soon. I cried with relief knowing that I had finally found my place in this world. My career choice was decided and although I would never, ever be the same again, I knew in my heart that *this* was what I was made for.

I realized what an impact my father's death had on me when, three years later, it became my practice as a paramedic to make sure that the patients who died in my care were presentable for their loved ones to see. I looked at them through the same lenses I had with my own father on the night he died. I always covered them with a blanket and left one of their hands resting on top for their loved ones to hold. There was always a chair and tissues nearby so the grieved could sit comfortably, for as long as they needed, as they said their goodbyes. Before bringing the bereaved in, I took a moment to explain what they would see and I gave them the opportunity to ask questions. I offered to go with them and I told them that it was okay to touch their loved one if they wanted to. Sometimes, I just sat with them in the silent darkness of their grief and held their hand. Other times, I simply stood beside them as they cried. I did all of this because I too have stood in this place and I know that there are times when words are not enough. These are the habits I still practice today.

On the first day of college, I felt I was in way over my head. I was one of the only high school grads in attendance, the rest of the class were mature students or graduates with one or more degrees. Leading up to that first day of school, I heard many times that I was too young, too small, too female. I had my work cut out for me because there was no plan B and I couldn't afford to fail. It's incredible what you can do when failure is not an option. Although the days sometimes felt like an eternity, the year passed quickly. Before I knew it, I was writing the entrance exam for Toronto Ambulance, and then I was walking through the doors on my first day as a new employee. *I made it!*

I didn't realize at the time what "making it" actually entailed. I knew I had entered a male-dominated career, a "boys club," if you will. For years, on each and every shift I had to prove that I could lift, that I was tough enough, smart enough, and capable enough until finally, the guys got to know who I was and what my abilities were. Acceptance came slowly and I had to have patience. I also had to develop a tough skin to deal with the daily come-ons or the snide remarks from colleagues, allied services, nurses, and even from my patients: "They let women do this job now?" or "I would NEVER let my husband work with someone like you!" Along with acceptance came camaraderie and, with time, the guys started to stand up for me. I spent the first fifteen years of my career being the only female on my shift. By that time, I had a band of brothers who helped and supported me as one of their own.

Throughout the years, I have had the opportunity to work in many divisions: Ceremonial Unit, Peer Support Team, Advanced Care Paramedicine, Public Safety Unit, CBRNE Team (Chemical Biological Radiological and Explosive), and Community Medicine. I became an acting superintendent and I have had the opportunity to teach and mentor employees. I have taken my skills on three medical missions: twice to the Democratic Republic of Congo and once to Zambia in 2020. When there were opportunities, I took them. I didn't let my gender or size stand in my way—I just went for it.

I am certainly not the same girl who started this career thirty-one years ago: I have seen things that can never be erased; I have heard things that still send chills down my spine; I have smelled things that have imprinted in my brain, and I have had to do things that will stay with me forever. This career has made its mark on my heart and soul, but I have never once regretted my decision to become a paramedic. This job continues to ground me in a way nothing else can and I am constantly left with a sense of gratitude for all that I have. I try to never take my days for granted because I have learned that life is precious and it can be taken in a moment. I have witnessed life slip away and I have been present as new life takes flight.

I have also been blessed with one of the greatest gifts of all: the fulfillment of my desire to be able to save another father in the way I was unable to save my own. One day I received a call for a patient who had a cardiac arrest in front of his wife. My partner and I were able to bring him back to life and get him the care he needed. This patient happened to be a friend of a friend who was able to find out who ran the call and contacted me personally. Over the next several months, I was kept informed of the progress this patient was making. Then one day, the man called to ask for the opportunity to meet and thank me in person. He shared that his youngest daughter was going to be married and invited me to the wedding. I attended this wedding and watched through tear-filled eyes as this father and his beautiful wife walked their radiant daughter down the aisle on one of the most important days of her life. I stood there, resting in the realization that she would never have to know what it was like to not have her father stand beside her and share in this wondrous milestone.

Life for me has finally come full circle . . . all is well.

Chapter 5

Own Your Magic

Rebecca Russell

"We are all connected, we all matter. Truth. But if you don't take the time to know, love, and understand yourself first, how will you know the best way to serve others?"

Growing up, Rebecca imagined she would be a social worker or a teacher. A former travel agent, stay-at-home mom, published Romance author, and hockey player, she figured she'd explored every facet of herself and what she could do. However, at fifty-eight years old, she was introduced to doTERRA, an essential oils company with an amazing philanthropic practice. Rebecca saw an opportunity to combine her love of teaching with her desire to make a difference. She embraced her next chapter and became a business owner. That's how her wellness company, Hope Essential, LLC was born. Intent on empowering others, Rebecca enjoys the roles of essential oils educator, author, and speaker. She is also passionate about spreading the message that Type 2 Diabetes is often preventable and reversible, naturally, through food and lifestyle changes. Driven by the belief that everyone deserves to age with quality of life, Rebecca eagerly shares her knowledge and experiences with others. Her tagline, "Choose you, choose natural, choose now," sums up her philosophy about life and health!

Still a fan of travel and adventure, she also enjoys long Harley rides in the beautiful Tennessee mountains with her husband of thirty-nine years. Rebecca's super-power is connectedness, and she creates a sense of family wherever she goes. She enjoys meeting new people and would love to hear your story!

hopeessential.com

ig: beckyrussellhopeessential ~ fb: BeckyRussellHopeEssential

When did you first know that you were different? Was that uniqueness celebrated? Did it make you feel like you were wrapped in a warm, cozy blanket of approval? Or, did that realization leave you feeling "less than," as if something were wrong with you?

I'll never forget picture day in first grade. I had worn my favorite dress with various shades of red and blue stripes. Just before I opened the car door to race into school, my mom suggested I smile with my mouth closed. Her words weighed on my heart and mind all day. *How* exactly did one smile with closed lips? Would all the other kids smile that way, too? What was wrong with my mouth? When picture time finally arrived, a million knots played tug-of-war in my stomach. The fear of smiling "wrong" produced the most pitiful picture. Hurtful nicknames soon followed: "Bucky Becky" and "Four Eyes." At times, I carried the weight of the world on my little shoulders.

At home, I both loved and dreaded the times when extended family gathered to watch slides. We projected images onto a bare wall, reliving holidays while sharing laughter, buttery popcorn, and sodas. But whenever a picture of me popped up on the screen, I'd hear a collective sigh, which I understood to mean, "Poor Becky with her buck teeth and thick glasses." I can't say for sure if those words were ever said out loud, but *something* gave me that impression and fed my insecurities about my appearance.

Overall, though, my childhood was pretty amazing. My parents were happily married. They provided us with what we needed and often more, through their hard work and knowing how to stretch a dollar. They lived their values and encouraged me and my siblings to be and do our best. I never doubted that I belonged—the ties were strong between generations. Even so, one fact remained: I. Was. Different. I didn't resemble anyone in my family, especially my mom, who had a large frame, round face, dark hair, hazel eyes.

I was slender, of average height, with a long, narrow face, blue eyes, and brown hair. Nor did I think and act like others in my family. I alone adored books, my parents surrounded themselves with lots of people, while I preferred the company of books and music. My parents had no idea how to handle such a serious, sensitive child.

Growing up, I took for granted that I was loved, and presumed that families were always safe and nurturing. (When I moved away, I discovered that's not a given for everyone.) Even though I never doubted my family's love for me, I dwelled on not being understood or accepted by the people who mattered the most to me. That ache in my heart prompted me to turn inward and find comfort and escape in fiction novels. The Boxcar Children and Nancy Drew mysteries often featured exotic locations and unusual characters who possessed individual strengths and weaknesses, and who struggled with common issues such as divorced parents and sick loved ones.

I understand now, that despite my young age, I was learning about personal development through reading the words on those pages. That knowledge empowered me to embrace my unique self. Nancy Drew never apologized for being smart and clever, she had a thirst for adventure, jetted around the world, and never let fear stop her from helping someone. I wanted those things, too!

I learned so much about human behavior, about myself, through reading fiction. If books were my first taste of magic, becoming a travel agent soon after high school and seeing the world was my second. I don't think it was a coincidence that I chose that occupation. Each novel planted the seeds for adventure in my mind. I pinched myself to make sure I wasn't dreaming when I walked the snow-covered streets of Salzburg and cruised the Greek Islands.

While the teasing about my appearance made my grade-school years difficult, that changed after eighth grade when the braces came off and contact lenses replaced the glasses. Unfortunately, jealousy caused other issues. Still, those challenging times led me to my love of reading and the subsequent initiation into personal growth. I am so grateful that I developed a strong sense of self early on. But what if you weren't so lucky? Is it too late?

Absolutely not! If you're feeling stuck and wondering where you fit in, the underlying cause might be that you don't know who you are. For many who struggle with belonging or purpose, the first instinct is to look outward for ideas. What are your friends doing? What or who is popular? But here's the real answer: our belonging is not dependent on whether others accept us, but whether we accept ourselves.

I also believe that before you can accept yourself, you need to know and understand yourself. I've created a formula to help you embrace what makes you unique—what I like to call your "magic"—so that you can figure out your purpose, and shine.

Self-awareness + Self-acceptance + Self-love = Living Your Purpose

Self-awareness: In my early thirties, I once again found myself not fitting in. Although I was blessed and thankful to be an at-home mom, I needed more. No other moms in my circle shared this struggle or the guilt. After endless episodes of *Sesame Street*, my brain screamed for stimulation. I hoped the answer might be a creative writing class at a community college, but I was daunted to find that the course had been mislabeled and was "How to Write a Novel."

God tricked me. Writing a novel proved extremely challenging and heart-breaking, yet exhilarating and fulfilling. I knew I was living my dream when I would get so lost in my fictional world that two hours would pass in what felt like ten minutes.

While I found acceptance and friendships amidst writers, I didn't fit that mold, either. Most knew they wanted to write books from the time they could read. Not me. Even so, I had hoped to publish many romances, for sure more than the two books with Harlequin Silhouette, but God had other plans.

While writing, another blessing that came my way was the book *Personality Plus* by Florence Littauer. A gift from a neighbor to help with creating characters, it also profoundly changed *my* life. I discovered that when we understand our inner selves, we can then work on being our best selves. The four temperaments—Sanguine, Choleric, Melancholy, and Phlegmatic—are tools for a deep dive into the examination of self. I discovered that being the sole Melancholy in a family of Sanguines and Phlegmatics was the only thing "wrong" with me. And as that sense of self-awareness grew, I could see others through a kinder lens, offer them acceptance, grace, even forgiveness.

Self-acceptance: I believe that self-acceptance must happen before change can occur. If you are not confident in who you are, doubt and insecurity will keep you stuck in fear. A book that was instrumental in my self-acceptance journey was StrengthsFinder 2.0 by Tom Rath. In this book, Rath expands upon the assessment tool called CliftonStrengths. The purpose of this assessment is to help you find areas where you have the greatest potential to develop strengths, instead of the more traditional goal of building up your weaknesses, which takes a lot more effort and energy.

Until I took the StrengthsFinder quiz, I had no idea connectedness was a strength! I saw my desire to create a sense of family wherever I am as a quirk instead of my super-power. I've created a vibrant, supportive community online for my customers and business partners. My strengths are my secret sauce. No one else can do me.

Self-love: I warn you: The gut-wrenching, not-sure-I-can-survive-this work is essential to the pursuit of self-love. Getting a grip on the first two concepts—self-awareness and self-acceptance—provides a strong foundation for the third.

Although I didn't have deep tragedy or trauma as a child or young adult, my scars are real and heavy to me. I've worked extremely hard at overcoming my dread of the camera. Even though I've had a beautiful smile most of my life now, I sometimes still hear the name-calling in my head. I've also dealt with fears around belonging and perfectionism, among others.

Self-love is a deep dive into healing. It's difficult to move forward while weighed down with old baggage. There's no magic wand to wave and make it all vanish. *The Self-Guided Guru* by Violette deAyala and *Judgment Detox* by Gabrielle Bernstein were part of my healing journey. I'll be honest, doing the exercises recommended in these books sometimes felt like rubbing salt into a wound. Counseling and other modalities are great choices for healing, too. But denial and avoidance are traps. You'll keep making the same mistakes, experiencing the same pain, until you deal with it. All. Of. It. Then you can own your truth.

You deserve success, joy, peace—to love and be loved.

Self-love is not selfish. Once we truly love ourselves, we feel so generous and free, that we're ready to encourage and lift up *others*. The healing can take time, but that's all the more reason to get started. Today.

Purpose: At the age of fifty-eight, I was content with my full-time office job and treating my essential oils business like a hobby. And then the unimaginable happened—I was fired! Completely unexpected! Utterly humiliating! Absolutely necessary! I guess God had grown tired of waiting for me to put my dreams first.

I threw myself into my essential oils business, determined to succeed but full of uncertainty. Fortunately, doTERRA is a personal development company wrapped in an essential oil company. I absorbed recommended webinars and podcasts that encouraged big dreams. I read *Secrets of the Millionaire Mind* by T. Harv Eker and embraced the truth that the more successful I am, the greater impact I can make.

My message of hope and healing needs to reach as many people as possible. Owning a wellness company is the perfect platform for expanding my reach. My big dreams include crushing it in a TED Talk and publishing a non-fiction book about holistic wellness. That magical flow I used to experience when writing fiction now happens during wellness consultations when an hour turns into two because we're having fun getting to know one another and setting health goals.

Health matters.

Several of the women in my family developed Type 2 Diabetes in their forties. One aunt died at sixty, my mom at sixty-nine, both from complications of diabetes. Repeatedly, I was seen but not heard as I tried to share information that might have helped them. I felt helpless watching them struggle and die too soon.

When at thirty-five I was diagnosed as pre-diabetic, fear and panic consumed me. Fortunately, a holistic practitioner guided me out of fear and into empowerment. With quality supplements and acupuncture, my numbers improved without medications. I haven't tested pre-diabetic for almost twenty years! When I discovered essential oils, my health up-leveled.

Now, because of my growing confidence and clarified vision, my goals have expanded, too. I'm so excited to share with the world what has helped me avoid Type 2 Diabetes, despite my genetic makeup. I couldn't save my family, but I am determined to share my wellness message with as many people as possible, especially those dealing with autoimmune illnesses. They—you—need to know that while no magic pill exists to restore your health, there is hope of reversing many autoimmune diseases, and in particular, Type 2 Diabetes.

In this season of my life, I am once again seen as different and sometimes even dangerous, because of my message of hope. I dare to question the standard approach to disease treatment, which often manages illness instead of building health. Thankfully, I am not alone in this cause. More and more experts are seeing the value of a holistic approach to wellness.

What makes me unique—my magic—has been the driving force my entire life, whether or not I was aware of it. I'm so blessed to not only know my purpose, but to pursue it. Most days I find myself grinning and thinking, *I can't believe this is my life*!

But how does this help you if you have no idea what your purpose is? Hang on, I've got your back!

In my humble opinion, purpose, as an adult, will most likely be found by going back to the beginning. All my life, I assumed I would be a teacher or a social worker, and it never happened the way I imagined. Instead, I now teach others about essential oils and a holistic lifestyle. I teach empowerment classes in my community. I have the perfect partnership with a heart-driven global company that shares my values and beliefs. And isn't a key component of social work the desire to make a difference?

So, what did you dream of doing or being as a child? Does that still appeal to you? If not, let your imagination run wild. Grab a book to help you discover your purpose. Two of my favorites are Wishcraft by Barbara Sher, and Dan Miller's 48 Days to the Work You Love. Listen to podcasts, attend workshops. Surround yourself with positive, supportive people.

Please don't take time for granted and remain stuck. You'll continue to age even if you don't learn a new skill or try something new. I am proof that you're never too old to start over.

Own your magic. Then freely share your unique gifts and talents. The world desperately needs all the love and magic we can offer. The world needs the magic of you.

Chapter 6

Authentically Evolving

Sylvia Calleri

"If you're not growing . . . you're dying."

As a Life Mastery Consultant, Sylvia can help you design and manifest a life that's in harmony with your authentic self and your soul's purpose. For over thirty-two years, Sylvia has worked as a media consultant, helping businesses with their sales and marketing strategies to build their dreams, accelerate their results, and create richer, more fulfilling lives. She is the proud mother of two adult sons who she adores. She feels blessed for the amazing circle of friends that surround her.

As a sought-after life coach and professional speaker, Sylvia offers inspiring workshops and retreats online and globally, as well as transformational in-depth coaching programs that help clients achieve new heights of success, meaning, and spiritual aliveness. Now combining this background with the proven Life Mastery technology, Sylvia is helping clients achieve extraordinary results in accelerated time. She is filled with joy and gratitude as she works with people to transform and close the gap between the life they're living and a life they'll love.

Sylvia offers content-rich interactive workshops that take participants on a journey in which they design, define, test, and experience a crystal clear vision of the life they will love—a life that is in alignment with their highest purpose. They have a unique opportunity to "step into" the life they are imagining and feel a resounding "yes."

authenticallyevolving.com

ig: authenticallyevolving ~ fb: Authentically Evolving by Sylvia

When I reflect upon my childhood, I must say, it was pretty good. I had two loving parents who adored each other. My father was a quiet man for the most part and loved his garden. He was a hard worker and I respected the entrepreneurial spirit that he passed down to me and my siblings. He was always looking for ways to make extra money. I didn't realize the impact my father had on me until later in life.

My mother was the strongest woman you could ever know. She was a talented seamstress and took on any DIY challenge around the house. She had the bluest eyes and a smile that would light up a room. She was always very warm and welcoming to anyone who entered her home and you never left on an empty stomach. I was the youngest of three children, each of us born five years apart. My sister, who was the eldest child, practically raised me. She married when she was sixteen years old and had a turbulent marriage. My brother, the young-boxer-turned-Elvis-impersonator, was the apple of my parents' eyes. Me, well, believe it or not, I was the quiet one. There was so much going on in our household that I preferred being in my room with my nose stuck in a book. Being from an Italian background, we believed it was important to keep up good appearances. Life centered around concerns over what other people would think. Problems were never discussed or dealt with. This behavior carried on into most of my life as I often worried about what people thought about me and how they perceived me. At home, I felt I had to dim my light and keep my parents happy as they were dealing with all of my sibling's problems. At school, I shone brightly. I was in the drama club and in school plays, elected vice president of the student council, awarded the Moriama Toshiba Award for Most Likely to Succeed, and played basketball and volleyball.

I was determined to make something of myself and be and do better. I took summer and night school courses to get ahead and finished high school early. I started my first part-time job at the age of twelve. I looked and acted a lot more mature than I was and was often mistaken as being older.

People who know me would say that if you want something done, I was the person to ask. When I put my mind to something, I made it work. I am a doer who takes action. This may be a positive thing for the most part, but it has gotten me into trouble because I don't think before acting. *Best to ask for forgiveness than permission.* What is interesting is that this theory worked in most areas of my life, except when it came to weight loss. This is a struggle I am still working on.

Fast forward into adulthood: I married my high school sweetheart; we were so in love before marriage. We had the typical big Italian wedding with three hundred guests and all the trimmings. We had a few blissful years together and then it went downhill slowly, like water draining from a clogged sink. I had it all—a gorgeous husband, two beautiful sons, a big home, and a successful career. So why was I so unhappy?

After having my sons at the age of thirty, I became clinically depressed. I gained weight and it took everything in me to get out of bed each morning to get my boys to school. I was going to the gym, practicing yoga, and seeing a counselor. No one understood why I continued to feel depressed, least of all me. Doctors were prescribing all kinds of meds for depression. At this point, I was thirty-two and had lost my menstrual period. I was not sleeping, was lethargic, moody, hot and cold, etc, etc. If these symptoms sound familiar to you, you've probably gone through menopause, but, at thirty-two, I thought I was going crazy.

Who would have thought I was going into premature menopause at such a young age. I thanked God I'd had my children when I did. While my friends around me were living it up, I was dragging my feet but had to show up for work like nothing was wrong. (Luckily, I took drama in high school.) Today, when I hear my friends complain about their hot and cold flashes and insomnia, it brings me back to a dark place, one I thought there was no way out of. Thankfully, I overcame the darkness I felt while experiencing menopause, but it took years. During that time, my husband was not very compassionate or supportive. It must have been frustrating for him to see me this way, knowing that I'd been vibrant and ambitious when we married. I tried hard to better myself since I often felt unworthy of his love. I filled my life with "busyness." I was a successful sales representative and earned awards and trips, and I had a part-time business doing home parties with lingerie and jewelry. I kept busy, but I was not fulfilled.

During those years, I used journaling to try to understand my feelings and revisited my older journals from ten years prior to realize that *nothing* had changed. Living in an unhappy and loveless marriage truly made me sad and was not good for my mental health. I still cared for my husband and truly wanted to make it work. I told him either we work at making our marriage better or work on ending it. His response was, "At the age of forty-five, I am who I am, take it or leave it." At the time, I thought what he said was harsh and hurtful because I believed he did not want to fight for us. That is what I was doing for so many years, but he was clear in telling me that he wasn't willing to work together and make any changes to improve our marriage. In the end, my choice to be happy led to the dissolution of our twenty-one-year marriage. Today, I am thankful for his clarity. By telling me he wasn't willing to change, he saved me from spending another ten years still living a passive, unhappy life.

So, What Next?

I have always considered myself to be positive and independent, and thought, "I can handle this." So I bought an older home and had it renovated. It was hard at first to make big decisions on my own. As you know, life will challenge you in ways you never thought possible. With the sudden death of my father, taking care of my sick mother, raising two teenage boys, having the financial burden of a household, and other health issues that kept arising, it became overwhelming and hard to manage it all. The death of my mother did me in. Driving home from the hospital after visiting with her, I almost fell asleep at the wheel, which scared the living daylights out of me. I knew then that I needed to take care of myself and I took some time off from my job. I recognized that I was starting to spiral into depression again and began to feel the same way I had years ago. To top it off, shortly thereafter, I fell and was immobile for ten months after breaking my knee and ankle. It felt like my world was crumbling around me. When this happened, I was building my beach house up north, and I had to pick out construction products online while confined to a chair. I kept asking, "Why me? What is the lesson in all of this? What message am I supposed to receive?"

It was a difficult and frustrating time. When I think back, I wonder how I did it and how it all came together so beautifully. It was not an easy time but, you know what, I got through it. I believe that things happen for a reason, although the reasons can be hard to understand at times. I now know that the lesson I needed to learn was that no matter how bad it gets, the darkness will pass and make you stronger. In the past when I prayed, I asked to not experience pain and heartache. Now I ask for the strength to get through it.

The Glimmer of Light

Over the years, I attended personal development courses and had a longing to get more out of life. I was searching for happiness and a sense of fulfillment. Have I found it? I'm still on my journey and am loving it! What I realized in the past year while dealing with this pandemic is that I have to start living the life I would love—now! Not when I lose weight or when I can afford it or when the boys are settled or when, when, when . . . I always had a longing to be and do more. I felt like I wasn't living up to my potential in life, which made me feel sad.

It's not that I wasn't appreciative of what I had in my life, as I am so blessed and feel very privileged to have accomplished so much. I thank God each and every day for my family and the amazing circle of friends that surround me and have always been there in my life to support me and pick me up when I am down. (You know who you are.)

What I do know for a fact is that I enjoy being involved in helping others. Whether I achieve this through involvement in my church, in women's groups, or as the chair of my kid's PTA, I have always known, down deep inside, that I had a longing to help others. It was in uncovering this light that I evolved and helped myself.

It gives me great pleasure and joy when helping others design a life they'd love to live. This is when I saw my light and decided to become a Certified Lifemastery Coach. I am in a place where I want to live as my authentic self and help others do the same. I think we evolve each day as we experience new situations that have hidden lessons in them. We all have a story to tell that makes us level up, be it by design or by default. Happiness is not a destination. It's a decision we each have to make for ourselves. I choose to be happy, even through challenging times. I start each morning in gratitude for what I have already accomplished and gratitude for all of the blessings coming my way. The ups and downs remind us we are alive, like the beeping of a heart monitor. Living on a flat line, or a mediocre life, isn't really living, it's existing. Building my resilience muscle to overcome any circumstance or situation is what keeps me driven so that I can help others do the same by leading by example. I welcome change as it helps me to grow and learn more about all that the Universe has to offer. Each day is a new beginning that offers lessons that cause us to evolve because of the new experiences that we go through. Having an open mind and heart helps and my faith in God keeps me grounded in comfort, knowing that I am not alone.

Chapter 7

Through Great Adversity Comes Great Strength

Molly Phair FNTP, CPT

"This wasn't something that was going to just go away overnight. It was something that I was going to have to be vigilant about for a lifetime. But it was worth it. My health and my life were worth fighting for."

Molly Phair is first and foremost a mother to four beautiful children and one fur baby, and wife to an amazing husband who puts up with all of her crazy! She is a lover of God, fitness, and food. Molly has a passion for helping others find their way through challenging health conditions using functional nutrition, supplementation, and lifestyle change. She is a Functional Nutritional Therapy Practitioner, NASM Certified Personal Trainer, and loves pumpkin pie, basketball, reading, music, and hanging out with her family. She lives in Meridian, ID, and runs her virtual Nutritional Therapy Practice (Phair Phitness & Nutrition) from home.

mollyphairphitness.com

ig: phairphitness ~ fb: phairphitness

li: Molly Phair

I remember it clearly. The day my life turned upside down. It was Thanksgiving Day, 2008. That was the day that I began to live in my little version of hell.

It began as something that seemed regular and routine. I had what I thought was a yeast infection. It was uncomfortable of course, but I did what I had always done. I went to the doctor, got some antibiotics, and went on my merry way. My symptoms soon subsided and all was right with the world.

Then in December, symptoms returned. I went to the doctor again, received more antibiotics, and you guessed it . . . my symptoms subsided.

From there, everything started to go a little haywire. My "yeast infection" was actually a chronic bacterial infection and what should have been taken care of quickly through antibiotics, seemed to spiral out of control. I experienced cyclical bacterial infections despite the constant and repeated use of antibiotics. Soon my symptoms intensified and spread to other parts of my body and mind.

Despite the efforts of my well-intentioned doctor, who continued to try every kind of antibiotic with me, I experienced a hot mess of symptoms including chronic migraines, intense fatigue, embarrassing digestive problems, psoriasis flares, bouts of debilitating anxiety and depression, year-long allergies, unexplained weight gain, brain fog, and more.

I was miserable. I hated what I saw in the mirror and how I felt physically, spiritually, and mentally. I struggled to show up for my four young children. It was nearly impossible to be there for my husband when he got home from work. And intimacy? Forget about it. It was painful and something I wanted to avoid at all costs. We lovingly referred to my lady parts as "the ring o' fire!" It was affecting every aspect of my life. It plagued me with an overwhelming feeling of hopelessness, not knowing what to do or where to turn for help.

I continued to see my doctor. She wanted to help me but had a limited number of tools in her tool belt—for two and a half years she prescribed me antibiotics and more antibiotics. She didn't know what else to suggest. During that time, I continued to get worse. Some days, I wondered how I would be able to face another day.

At this point, I knew I needed help beyond what the doctors could suggest and beyond what I could do for myself. I belong to the Church of Jesus Christ of Latter-Day Saints, and my husband, being a holder of the priesthood, was able to give me a priesthood blessing. In this blessing, I longed for relief. I wanted God to make me whole—to heal me—right then and there.

But He didn't.

Rather, in my blessing, he told me that I would need to endure a little longer, that I would need to search out alternative forms of healing. In my journey, He would lift me up and help me bear the burdens of increasingly poor health and mental instability.

Even though I was devastated in my heart, I had hope because I felt certain that with time and some effort, I would heal.

This is where the intense research began. I decided to do something bold and walk away from Western medicine. I knew there had to be alternatives and I was going to find them!

It wasn't long after my husband and I went down the internet rabbit hole that we found an online program that looked promising. The program used nutrition and supplementation to heal the body from chronic bacterial infections and yeast overgrowth. At the time we were very poor, and the cost of the program and supplements was around $600. We didn't have the money, but we did have the faith so we decided to pay with credit.

When I began the protocol, I was sick. I knew little about functional medicine and what was happening in my body. I didn't realize that my chronic overuse of antibiotics had created an antibiotic-resistant superbug in my gut and that all of my good gut bacteria was gone. Over time, this turned into a leaky gut, leaky brain, and a chronic weakening of my immune system. My body had a lot of healing to do. Even though the creator of the program warned us of the uncomfortable healing reactions our bodies would undergo,

I didn't expect to feel exhausted and nauseous every morning and night.

But I stayed the course. I took the supplements, radically changed my nutrition, and focused on rest, all while caring for my four kids. My husband was my biggest cheerleader. When I wanted to quit, he was there to help me keep going.

After about two months of religiously following the protocol, things changed. I woke up one morning feeling like a brand-new person! I felt like myself again. I had forgotten what it felt like to feel good. My energy skyrocketed, and I could make it through a day without having to lock myself in my room and lie down for a bit just to get through the rest of the day. I was down to my pre-wedding weight, my digestive problems subsided, my migraines were gone, my psoriasis went away, my allergies subsided, and I didn't have bacterial infection symptoms. It felt like a miracle had occurred!

From that point on, I became more familiar with functional medicine. I found a functional medicine practitioner in southern Oregon that I could work with, and my long-term healing journey began. This wasn't something that was going to just completely reverse direction overnight. It was something that I would have to be vigilant about for a lifetime. But my health and my life were worth fighting for. My kids deserved a mom that could show up for them physically, spiritually, and mentally. My husband deserved a wife who had the energy for date night, snuggles, and intimacy. And I deserved to feel healthy, happy, and whole!

This journey sparked something in me. At the time, I was working as a music therapist and teaching piano. However, this healing process had such a profound effect on me that I found a new passion for helping women find natural solutions to their health struggles. Rather than band-aid and symptom suppression solutions, I help women find ways to heal the body that won't simultaneously destroy it. It took me years to figure it out on my own, so I wanted to create a path for others that gave hope and healing. My hope is that they, too, can experience light at the end of the tunnel.

Looking back, I realize God had a plan for me. I wasn't supposed to be immediately healed. I was supposed to go through some suffering, to find a solution so I could then be a light for others.

I gained an understanding and empathy that I couldn't have acquired any other way. Now I am able to guide others out of what feels like a dark and hopeless tunnel to light and hope. It is my passion to help women become their own healthcare advocates and find a path to physical, spiritual, and mental health. I challenge them to never settle for feeling less than their best because they deserve it. Truly health is the best form of wealth!

In addition, I realize the importance of always caring for myself. For truly, to be a light to others, I myself must glow. In the gospel of Matthew, Jesus said: "Neither do men light a candle and put it under a bushel, but on a candlestick; and it giveth light unto all that are in the house." This is my passion and purpose. Out of my mess has come my message.

Thirteen years have now passed since that Thanksgiving Day and I am so grateful for the journey that has helped me to create a system for women to reclaim their right to vibrant health. My system is a simple step-by-step, progress over perfection approach that uses my six pillars of health (nutrition, exercise, hydration, sleep, stress management, and personal/spiritual development) and my six steps of success (mindset, habits/routines, guiding principles, accountability, planning in advance and tracking). This gives my clients a framework or foundation from which to build and customize their own unique system per their own individual goals, struggles, and needs.

I want this for you too! It is impossible for me to share my entire system with you in a chapter, but I can give you some simple action strategies. You can take these steps right now to experience some of your own transformational moments as you strive to regain your health and become the best version of yourself.

> Strategy #1: Write your vision. This is different from determining your goals. Your vision is what you want your life to look like in the future. It's much different than simply saying: "I want to lose twenty pounds" for example. Let's dig deeper. Why do you want to lose twenty pounds? How would losing twenty pounds impact your life and how you feel? Sit down

and allow yourself to get emotional and passionate about what you want for your future. Get as detailed as you can about how you want to feel, how it will affect your relationships, your finances, your work, how you see yourself in the mirror, and so forth. This is a critical step you can't skip because it will be the driving force that keeps you going when you are frustrated, overwhelmed, or struggling with a setback. Once you have completed your vision, schedule a few moments daily to read it and feel the emotion of it. Then let that emotion drive your action for the day. Your vision should be big and leave you feeling a little uncomfortable, but you should also believe that if you create the right action and habits in your life, you can absolutely accomplish it.

Strategy #2: After you have a very compelling and emotionally-driven vision, now you have to get real. Take a minute to do some self-reflection on where things are currently at for you. Don't try to sugarcoat it. I call this the Reality Check. The Reality Check gives us an opportunity to start with a point of reference so we can set some meaningful goals before acting. For my 1:1 clients and my Healthy Happy Whole community, I give them a worksheet that helps guide them through this process. Otherwise, it's just pen to paper! You got this!

Strategy #3: Congratulations! You know where you want to go and you have identified where you are right now. Now it's time to create a plan! Based on the information you have, how are you going to build a bridge from where you are right now to get you to where you want to go? A wise mentor once told me that action beats anxiety. A vision will only get us so far if we aren't willing to then take action. I like to teach my clients a simple ninety-day system for creating goals within which you can accomplish more in ninety days than many do in a year. I prefer this over setting annual goals because we aren't fortune tellers—we can't see that far into the future but we can plan out ninety days at a time with some certainty that we can follow through. In a nutshell, here is how you set up your first ninety-day plan.

Based on your vision, decide on one to three goals that will make the biggest impact on your life right now or that are the most meaningful to you. These can be physical, spiritual, mental, financial, relationship, business, etc. Make sure they are specific, measurable, and have a deadline.

After you have chosen your one to three things, break that down into a monthly plan. When writing your plan, ask yourself: what do I need to accomplish monthly to make my goals a reality?

Once you have created a monthly plan, break it down even further into the activity you need to take each week. Have a calendar handy! If you know what you need to accomplish monthly, what do you need to act on weekly in order to get there?

The hardest part is now over! The next step is to get it into your calendar. I use a time blocking system. To time block, simply look at your blank calendar and fill it in first with your non-negotiables like family time, self-care, and so forth. Then, fill in the rest with your weekly action items. Finally, you can fill in any other time blocks in the week with miscellaneous business or personal items. This way you ensure that the most important things get done!

Pro tip: To make sure that you act on your vision, goals, plan, and action steps, set aside thirty to sixty minutes a week to review your progress. Did you follow through with your weekly action plan? What were your wins? What were your struggles? Do you need to adjust anything for the new week? Remember, this is critical because creating lasting transformation in your life doesn't come from the things you do once in a while. It's what you do intentionally and consistently that makes the biggest difference!

Celebration time! At the end of every ninety days, it's important to take time off, evaluate your progress, and reward yourself for your success. You will use this time to create your next ninety-day plan. My husband and I like to plan a little weekend getaway where we take time together, regroup, recharge, and plan our next ninety days.

By following these guidelines, you will be amazed at the discipline and transformation that will take place.

Whether your goal is to transform your health, your business, or your relationships, it doesn't matter. It all comes down to the same critical, intentional action and it is what changed my life and my health.

Lastly, if you only walk away with one thing, please remember to never settle for feeling less than your best. Why? Because you deserve it and are worthy of it. And, you can do it! Don't let the dark moments of your life define you—let them change you!

Chapter 8

No Trespassing

Sonya van Stee

"Boundaries, like fences, are there for a reason and should be respected"

Aptly dubbed "The Effervescent Entrepreneur" during a radio interview some years ago, Sonya brings her positive "We'll figure something out" attitude everywhere she goes. She is a good listener, is eager to encourage, and loves inspiring others to be and to do better!

Sonya has a degree in education and a background in music and linguistics, and she is currently running a large dairy operation in Southwestern Ontario with her husband and his family. She has been in and out of network marketing for the past twenty-five years and is successfully building a global team in her current company.

Sonya and her tall Dutch farmer, Niek, have two indoor cats, an undetermined number of barn cats, and about 650 cows. They were unable to have children, but they spent time as foster parents and have considered adoption. In her spare time, Sonya enjoys reading, singing, cruising, and spending time outdoors by their country home.

ig: sonya_van_stee ~ fb: Sonya van Stee

As I sit here contemplating life, I am struck by words from an ancient text. You may recognize it: ". . . and forgive us our trespasses, as we forgive those who trespass against us."[1] We've all seen signs on old buildings or private properties that say "No Trespassing," but what does that really mean? Could it have a deeper meaning than simply: do not enter? Trespassing indicates that someone is crossing a boundary they are not authorized to cross.

My name is Sonya and I want to share with you a little snapshot of my life journey, specifically relating to a time I had to learn to forgive someone for trespassing. My words may be short, but the journey was nothing of the kind. What happened in just a few moments impacted me longer and in more ways than I could ever imagine.

Without getting into detail, a family "friend" sexually abused me when I was eleven years old. Twice: once in his home and once in mine. My mind went into shock. Did that really just happen? *What* exactly just happened? Was that my fault? What should I have done? What should I do now? So many questions came tumbling from my brain as I tried to make sense of things.

I probably should have said something to my parents or another adult I trusted. But who could I trust? Someone I thought I could trust had violated me. What if the person I chose to confide in didn't believe me or betrayed my confidence? Or worse, did the same thing as my attacker did? So I remained silent and hid everything in my mind and heart. For *ten years*.

I held in the feelings of guilt, betrayal, and shame and tried to move on with my life as if nothing had happened. Mysteriously, this is also the time that I developed a keen fear of the dark. It wasn't so much the darkness itself that scared me, but what might lurk *in* the dark waiting to harm me. Anyone who knew me as a youngster knows I was a carefree, happy, and trusting child. I was

1 Matthew 6:12-14 KJV

confident, sure of myself, and had joy enough to spread around to everyone I came into contact with . . . until that fateful day. Suddenly, I was self-conscious and didn't want anyone to notice me. I started pre-determining what kind of personality I would exhibit during events and gatherings. Sometimes I was the shy girl who stood in the corner and hoped to remain invisible; other times, I showed up as the boisterous, good-natured, fun-loving person I thought people wanted me to be. I felt this was the way to stay in control, but deep down I knew that neither of those personas was truly me.

As the weeks became months and my alter "personas" were living my life as a lie, I developed other fears and embarked on another destructive journey—this time it was my relationship with food that blossomed into a full-on eating disorder that I denied for many years. My eleven-year-old mind was convinced that if I started overeating and gaining weight, I wouldn't be attractive, men wouldn't notice me, and I would be safe. Food became both comfort and protection—not a healthy combination.

Fast forward to when I was twenty-one. I took a semester off college to travel with my parents and three youngest siblings. Things were a little rocky between my parents and me, but for some reason, I decided to unburden myself of the events from ten years prior. I gathered up every ounce of courage I could muster and told my parents what had happened. I expected an outburst of rage, or at the very least shock and concern for my well-being. I got nothing. *Nothing*! It shattered me. Was it all my fault after all? Was I making more of this than was necessary?

Should I have just kept my mouth shut? I had so many questions. All the old questions plus a myriad of new ones gushed out in a steady stream that soon became a churning river full of feelings of unworthiness, guilt, sadness, fear, and low self-worth. In response, I shut down even more . . . and ate. I hid candy and ate it secretly when nobody was around. I had always enjoyed sweets, but now I craved them more than ever. Eating sweets became my "happy place" while at the same time I knew intellectually that I was exhibiting destructive behavior. It was as if something was overpowering me, and I continued gaining weight (and hating myself for it).

I don't blame my parents for not knowing what had happened. They noticed a change in my eating habits, but it didn't occur to them that there was something much deeper that was showing up in my eating habits. They saw the symptom but not the root cause. When I was thirteen, my parents decided they needed to intervene with my eating and introduced me to dieting. Oh, the stories I could tell of diets! Over the years, I'm sure I've tried almost every single one. I can probably tell you every flavor of shake from every company out there. And don't get me started on the cabbage soup diet.

With each new program, I lost weight and then gained more after I stopped. I started believing that I could never be a "normal" weight, so I would give up. Then the shame would kick in again and I would try another diet. This constant yo-yo of weight loss and weight gain ate at the fibers of my soul. My self-esteem took beating after beating, and I felt more alone than ever before.

When I saw my reflection in the mirror, all I saw was disgust, guilt, and embarrassment scowling back at me. It was disheartening to not only feel those emotions, but to *see* them as well. It was as if my reflection were another person judging me. I felt unworthy, miserable, and perpetually guilty. It didn't matter that the circumstances that had led me to this point weren't my fault: I still felt shame.

So how did I drag myself (and I *do* mean drag; it was no easy feat) out of the depth of despair and the torment inflicted on myself because of my situation? That's a great question. It has taken me a *long* time to get to the place where I don't hate my reflection. I'm here to tell you that it *is* possible to love yourself, even when you've made mistakes. I think the biggest change has been finally seeing myself as worthy. I *am* worthy to be all that I was created to be. I *am* worthy to be the shape and size that God intended for me all along. I *am* worthy of being loved.

Another ten years passed before I mustered enough courage to broach the subject of abuse again with my parents. I was thirty-one years old and about to get married. I don't know what changed, but *this* time my parents reacted with outrage. My dad was ready to rush over to my assaulter's home and punch him in the nose, or worse. *Finally*, I felt vindicated. I wasn't wrong all those years. All my feelings were normal. So many feelings rushed to the surface, threatening to drown me in a sea of emotions. At the forefront was the question *why*? Why didn't you feel this way when I told you ten years ago? Why was today different? Why didn't you *ask* me why I suddenly refused to go near the man's house? Why didn't you ask me why I started eating so much, instead of just putting me on diet after diet that never worked? I had longed to say something, but I didn't know how. For so many years, all I wanted was for them to ask me what was going on. As I allowed myself to ask the questions, and with the reactions of my parents giving me a sense of closure, the healing could finally begin. With scars that had deepened with the years, healing would be long in coming. This would be no easy task.

Anyone who has been sexually assaulted understands that sometimes things trigger you that you never even thought about. Who knew that such a short period of time could affect so many areas of life and for so many years? I once received a poor grade in speech class and later realized that it was because of an unexplained nervousness toward the teacher, who resembled and exhibited some of the same mannerisms as those of my attacker. Add to that my fear of being noticed, and it was a recipe for disaster. I was still only a teenager, though, and I didn't have an understanding of what was going on until looking back years later. Perhaps a more obvious result was my shyness in being intimate with my husband. To this day, I still occasionally flinch at his touch; but I am determined that my past will not continue to affect our relationship!

A few years ago, my physician recommended I start to see a counselor to help me work through my trauma as well as the aftermath that I was still carrying. What a relief it was to share openly with someone who listened without judgment and with the sole purpose of helping me through the darkness and back to the light. Was it an easy process? Not even remotely! With her guidance and support, we revisited the trauma. In a way it was like reliving it, but as a spectator rather than a victim.

Through torrents of tears, she helped me to let go of the resentment, the shame, and the guilt I had been carrying for decades. I managed to do something I never thought I could—forgive him. It wasn't for him, though. It was for me. I needed to be free of him once and for all! I searched his name on the internet and found a photo of him. I opened up that photo, looked him square in the eye, and said, "I forgive you. Even though you never asked and probably don't deserve it, I forgive you."

At that moment, it was as if a giant, invisible burden dissipated off my shoulders, and I burst into tears. These tears were different; they were a sigh of relief as the world suddenly became brighter and more inviting again like it was when I was a child.

I would love to say that all my problems dissolved immediately along with the guilt and resentment, but almost three decades of emotional baggage and eating disorders don't just disappear overnight. We had torn down the structure I had built from shame, resentment, guilt, and fear. The foundation was damaged, but we patched it up with forgiveness. Now I could begin rebuilding with hope, love, and light.

The scars remain on the foundation as a reminder of my dark times, but they are no longer open, gaping wounds. I am at a place now where I can talk about my past. There are still tears, but I know that my past no longer defines me. I don't even think about my abuser anymore. Even in recounting this story, I no longer harbor any resentment or anger toward him. He doesn't hold any power over me, and he never will. That scared, helpless little girl of my past has transformed into a confident, strong woman who will not give in to the cowardly acts of abuse.

***

Several years ago, my husband and I decided to foster. After many weeks of questions, paperwork, and training, we were finally approved! Our lives changed dramatically as a sweet, beautiful six-year-old boy came into our care. This little man had suffered both physical and sexual abuse in his few short years, and my heart cried with his as he acted out in frustration when he didn't know how to express himself. "I understand, Little Munchkin, I understand. And I will love you no matter how you behave."

He was only with us for one year, but I know we were able to impact his life forever and that he will carry some amazing memories of our time together, just as we do!

Over the past several months, I have been privileged to find a coach/mentor who has taken me to the next level in personal development, especially in regard to my self-image. She taught me more about forgiveness, including forgiveness toward myself. I never even thought of forgiving myself! But as we dug deeper, I realized that I was still harboring a great deal of resentment, not to the man who started this whole scenario but to myself. I needed to forgive myself for being helpless, for not standing up for myself, for not telling anyone, for eating, for hating myself, and so many other things. The resentment still creeps up sometimes, but I'm on the right path.

My husband now says that I am a completely different person and that he is both happy for and proud of me. He has supported me for more than a decade, and I couldn't be more grateful for him. His patience and love, even through the rough times, have been my anchor. I wouldn't be where I am without him.

As I sit here contemplating life, I realize I am truly blessed. The things in my past no longer have a hold on me. I have people in my life who love me exactly the way I am. I can serve others through the pain and scars of my own background. The "trespasses" are forgiven, and I am free to be the person I was always meant to be!

Chapter 9

I've Been In There All Along

Helen Harwood Snell

"Change doesn't have to come through epiphanies, just as long as you get there."

Helen Snell is a content writer with a focus on storytelling. She is an international best-selling author and creator of the Story Business Mastery program. She teaches entrepreneurs the art of connecting their story with their client's story to create relationships that convert to sales. As a certified Communication Coach with Codebreaker Technologies, she further helps her clients understand how people hear their message.

Helen develops biographies, profiles, web content, and marketing materials that bring out the person behind the business. Her favorite work is ghostwriting blogs, books, and legacy stories. Her passion project is telling stories for the planet. She plans to ghostwrite stories of special needs adults to shine their light on the world.

When she's not writing or reading stories you will find her outside year-round. She is a true Canadian embracing all four seasons with equal enthusiasm. She is a single mother of three adult children and has learned some of her best life lessons from them. She embraces a plant-based lifestyle to live in harmony with the planet and is working towards living even more connected to the land on a small farm in rural Ontario.

helenharwoodsnell.com

ig: helenharwoodsnell ~ fb: helensnellstoryteller

li: Helen (Harwood) Snell

I spent so many years closed. I was closed to asking for help, to letting love in, and to who I was. I was always guarded in relationships, in business, and in trusting my intuition.

Picture this girl: green velvet dress and matching stockings, black patent-leather shoes, flaming red ringlets, chubby freckled cheeks smiling at the camera. There might have been a tooth missing. This is one of the first photos I remember where I wasn't myself. I hated sitting under the hairdryer on Saturday nights with my hair in little foam rollers. I hated dresses and leotards and all things girly. But there I sat, all tidied up in front of the piano I practiced daily, just like my mother wanted, for church or Christmas–whatever the occasion was. But all I wanted was to get dirty!

I grew up in the country and I was always outside. I still love earthy smells like fresh-cut grass and the forest after the rain. My hands were usually dirty as were the knees of my pants. I ate peas straight from our vegetable garden and caught whatever snakes and fireflies I could find. I gravitated to sports like baseball where I could slide in the mud—it was my absolute favorite to play in the rain. Even now, as I write this, I'm about to participate in a 5km mud run with a group of women from my online fitness community. That dirty kid is still in there, dying to get out!

As busy as I was outdoors, my mind was always busy, too. As a creative type, I have always had a mind full of ideas, graphic images, and creations. That busy imagination also developed fears which lead to a life of people-pleasing. It kept me from listening to myself; instead living to a standard that others set for me.

That lifelong journey of pleasing others made it easy to keep a part of myself closed. I did well in school and associated myself with academia. Something wouldn't allow me to fully step into that though, and I opted for college instead of university. I fell in love with an architectural drafting course in high school and started down the path of design and build. It was hands-on and I loved it.

In our third year, we had the opportunity to design a local library. The successful student would receive placement with a local architectural firm at graduation. That was real life. That made sense to me. I was one of five girls in a class of one hundred students. Instead of playing the odds in such a large dating pool, I became one of the boys and coached the boys' hockey team. My closed heart fit right in. I was awarded an opportunity to become employed right out of school through a government program featuring women in non-traditional roles. It took me into electrical drafting, so I followed that path. I took each opportunity that was presented to me. I became an expert. I trained others. I made visits to construction sites and engineering firms. At the young age of twenty-five, I was the national sales manager for an electrical product line. I never felt like I fit into that role. I thought it was because I was a woman, but I see now it was because it wasn't in my area of passion. Open doors but a closed heart once again.

I discovered many years later, in my mid-thirties, through a personality assessment that I was a "blue" nurturer who valued harmony over the "green" personality type represented by analytics and knowledge. I remember being angry. It was a group gathering of fourteen people and I admit with some embarrassment I kicked up a fuss. I wanted to be smart! I wanted to be green! (Kermit the Frog, anyone?) Intelligence was all I knew. But this provided the first step toward rediscovering the light I had buried. It was a small nudge that had me looking for that dirty, happy child.

I'm a slow learner in some ways. I've never chosen a solid career or had a wake-up call that pivoted my life in a single moment. Strangely, as much as I have been closed, I don't do well alone. I need community. I learn best when I share ideas with others. I find resonance with people and that inspires my thoughts and creativity. Change has been a slow burn for me for over twenty years.

That change began when my marriage started to shatter. I married someone I was unsure of because that was next on the list of things to do. I thought we had similar goals and common interests. It wasn't long before I found myself bending and eventually breaking to his wants and needs. I struggled for years to make it work. I shrunk even further from my true self. Faith was a haven where I found community and value. It was safe. I felt like I belonged. I could show the parts of me I wanted to show while hiding my insecurities and self-doubt in the cloak of prayer and spiritual awakening.

That concept of learning in a group environment is not lost on me. Faith was meant to be discussed in groups. Protests and movements only happen when people band together. Even family is supposed to be a safe place for the balance of self-expression and acceptance of others. But with everyone striving for some sort of Nirvana, to some degree, we have all become lost to our true selves. This leads to selfishness, addiction, mental health struggles, and a breakdown of community. For me, it created walls.

Years of self-doubt created distant friendships, but none too close. I cried quietly when I had a chance to be alone in a busy household. This stoicism served me well in the business world. I worked mainly with men for many years, and then managed a large business where I wore many hats and constantly kept my mind full of tasks. I had no time to be sensitive to my needs. I did find myself, however, being sensitive to the needs of others.

That sensitivity ramped up when I had children. I became hyper-sensitive with the birth of my third child. My oldest daughter was being bullied at her daycare and I had just delivered a beautiful baby girl with Down syndrome. My mother was dying. Life priorities changed. Management and high salary didn't matter. I left my job in order to show up fully for my family. Somehow being a full-time mother was even busier and left me empty and exhausted much of the time. I felt less of a partnership when I wasn't contributing financially. The walls rose higher. There was beauty and joy as well. I loved being a mother. It's hard for women to find a balance between parenting, work, and themselves. I made it harder because I refused to ask for help. It is said the inability to receive support from others is a trauma response. I somehow lived two lives—an independent life inside a marriage, and another surrounded by a loving extended group of family and friends. I believe that trauma, like it is for so many of us, was being closed, even to myself.

A few times, I had to walk away without knowing why. Once, I told my husband I needed a break. I booked a weekend trip to the big city all by myself. I felt a sense of adventure and self-assurance staying in that hotel in downtown Toronto. Cherished time was spent aimlessly walking through the shops and eating meals that I didn't make. My mind was just beginning to re-engage with my body when the weekend was over. But those awakened dreams lay just beneath the surface.

This past year sprouted so many of the seeds that were sown over decades. I love telling the stories of others. My business is writing for others, helping them discover their value so they can share it with the world. But I had never embraced my value. I've always been a helper, working in the background to lift others, making events happen, shining the light on someone else. The idea of uncovering my light was a slow discovery, like everything else in my life. I didn't feel I had a brilliant light hiding under some dark cover. But I've experienced a shift in embracing the light that others saw in me, like a flickering candle. The quiet, steady, thoughtful presence that others gravitate to in times of crisis.

In 2001 my ladies' baseball team was set to head to Niagara Falls, Ontario for the provincial finals. We questioned going at all, as it was only two short weeks after 9/11 and not too many miles north of New York. That playoff weekend was always balanced with competition and fun but the somber events curbed the playfulness that particular year. Four of us chose to go a few days early to golf. We wanted to support the economy that had been devastated. On the golf course, getting warmed up for the weekend, the conversation touched on the recent tragedy and our response to it. My friends knew I attended church but never asked a single question about my faith in the past. Now my opinion mattered. My perspective in a world of light and darkness suddenly had a personal connection to them.

During the recent pandemic, some friends did the same thing. Knowing my stance on our government's unhealthy approach to pharmaceuticals and food, they asked for advice on how to process the changing information on lockdowns and experimental vaccines. I don't push my opinions on people. I never have. In circumstances like these, I lead with empathy but I share cold, hard facts. I don't need to be heard. You won't find me on a platform very often, but I will share my knowledge when it's important. Two things that are very important to me are harmony and truth. I embraced harmony many years ago after accepting that somewhat traumatic "blue" personality analysis. It has built over time to be one of my main drivers. It took writing this chapter to realize that the harmony I seek is the light I hold against the darkness of deception. I had never called it advocacy before. But that's what I was stepping up to own. The mama bear that reared up when my youngest was born has continued to advocate for her and her community ever since. I have been an advocate for youth, for the planet, and for freedom of autonomy and speech in Canada.

My advocacy shows up as sharing information. I have enjoyed teaching throughout my life, whether at work or finding new ways to teach my daughter to address her learning needs. Learning is like breathing for me. And the best way to learn is to teach. I can't imagine that part of me ever being closed. The fact that an airplane can fly or that trees communicate with one another still teases my imagination with child-like wonder. I always have to be learning something. It might be that smart "green" part of me that I want to hold onto. Teaching what I learn has always been a part of myself I could share. It's separate from me. It's data. It doesn't have feelings or doubts. It serves that closed part of me.

Or does it? There has been a change in how data is accepted in the world. As people are more separated from their true selves, they are also that much more offended by opinions different than their own. A difference of opinion is seen as a line in the sand. Emotions rise and facts don't matter. Families and friends have been broken apart by different opinions. Schools and governments attempt to conform us to one line of thought. And recently when those thoughts don't align social channels are blocked or manipulated.

During these two years in and out of lockdown, I began to embrace my inner light. I spent a good part of 2020 uncovering information in shared circles. I researched government and alternative data. I fact-checked. But the science we were pressured to believe was winning because free speech was being reduced. This became the catalyst that fired me up to stand firm in my beliefs, but it came at a cost. That closed part of me was now open and vulnerable. My closed and distant approach to advocacy was personal. In the early months of 2021, I became utterly overwhelmed with what felt like the futility of my efforts. A long lockdown in Ontario took its toll. I became depressed for the first time in my life. I was no stranger to the pattern. I watched helplessly as others close to me had suffered through depression for years, but it was new to me. I ate poorly. I even reverted occasionally from my plant-based diet. I was disgusted with myself and falling deeper into patterns of self-sabotage. That change in diet was in part because depression stole away my desire to cook. I have enjoyed cooking and baking since I was ten years old. Suddenly I had no desire. I didn't want to cook for myself or others. We ordered lots of takeout food and I gained weight. I became inconsistent with my fitness, and even, at times, my hygiene. My health and wellness business struggled because I felt like a fraud. I lost clients due to my inability to sell myself as an ambassador of health. It felt like that business was going to die just like so many others had during the pandemic. I self-isolated and spent a lot of time fighting with my thoughts.

With the hope of spring, I spent a lot of time in my garden and felt some measure of life returning to my low energy in 2021. But the desire to cook didn't return. The depression hung on. I continued to research and share information on human rights and freedom of choice, but nothing felt whole. I realized I wasn't whole. I wasn't even excited about harvesting my garden. I froze most of it. Summer turned into fall and, with that, I took several steps that flooded me with much-need serotonin. I sold my home to be free of debt. I asked for help and became clear on my business and life goals. A balance of faith and energy work started to connect me back to my true self. I felt free. I was free of both debt and judgment. Finally, I could make the choices I needed to make. I was moving back to a connection with nature and living sustainably. I was ready to get dirty.

I found my voice for many years as an advocate because I wanted to speak for future generations. Just like writing for others was easier, so was speaking up for others. But those years of quiet taps on the shoulder were awakening my inner voice, too. I stepped into my needs in a new way. I found that little spark that had been hiding deep inside and I let it grow into a beautiful glow. I gave time to people and projects that inspired me and walked away from others. I finally put my voice in print.

I had lived my life prepared for heartbreak and disappointment. I didn't feel worthy of love. I didn't know who I was or what I wanted. When I was vulnerable, I was disappointed. I didn't trust others and I didn't trust myself either. I was afraid to speak up or stand out. The slow journey of re-discovering myself through helping others finally became real. I trust myself now and that has allowed me to be open. I am now open to new experiences, friends, and unconditional love. I'm ready to get dirty again. With age and experience comes wisdom, but also the light.

Chapter 10

From Burnout to Rediscovery

Laura Dawson-McCormack

"For years, I had been looking at success the wrong way. And it took a full-blown global pandemic to make me slow down and reconnect with who I truly am. I decided to change how I was living my life. I decided to see my worth as Laura, rather than my job title."

Laura Dawson-McCormack is a hospitality professional and certified life coach who graduated from the University of Guelph with a Bachelor of commerce. When Laura isn't working, she can be found curled up with her two cats, meditating, taking a walk by the water, or listening to music.

ig: lauradawsoncoaching

There I was sitting in the middle of a giant conference room, secretly praying to see my name appear on the screen. My heart was pounding, I had butterflies in my stomach, and I held my breath in anticipation . . . Yes! There it was! There was an eruption of applause and cheers. Everyone stood up around me and offered high-fives, hugs, and pats on the back in celebration. I had done it! My restaurant had just won the top award in my company for guest experience. With each step towards the stage, I reminisced over all the challenging shifts I overcame, all the late nights and long hours, and all the personal growth that I needed to do to get here. I approached the stage, standing tall, beaming with pride, and I accepted the award graciously. This was the recognition that I had been waiting for. I finally felt accomplished. I finally felt successful. But most importantly, I finally felt worthy.

My story begins at twenty-six when I started my career as a general manager in the corporate restaurant world. Being a recent graduate, I was on a mission to find my big girl job to cross off one of the important to-dos in my life. At the time, I was inexperienced with managing a business, but I was ambitious and determined to prove that I was the right woman for the job. When I began my career, I walked into the role with confidence. During the first year, I presented myself in a very specific and strategic way that mirrored my previous managers. I made sure I was serious, strict, analytical, and even a little intimidating at times. This is how I thought I needed to act in order to be successful. But deep down, I knew those actions felt cold, robotic, and inauthentic. During those first few years, I stumbled through my role and it reflected in my performance. But, I made sure that I learned from my mistakes. I worked twice as hard to redeem myself of any shortcomings. The investment and effort seemed worth it at the time because I was doing it with one goal in mind: to be successful in my career.

Fast forward four years and there I was, standing on that stage with an award in my hand. This was about much more than just an award. This was a milestone! It represented my transformation from the brand new twenty-six-year-old general manager into an accomplished businesswoman. I returned to work feeling fired up with this award in hand. But, after a few weeks, I noticed I had lost that momentum. All I could think was, "Ok, now what?"

Feeling stalled in my career, I decided I needed to embrace a new challenge, so I threw my name in for an upcoming restaurant opening. Now I had a new goal to work towards: to do what I did the first time around, except better and faster.

When it came time for this new restaurant opening, I started to do what I did the first time around. I put in the long hours; I brought home the extra workload; I answered late-night phone calls, and invested all my time and energy into training this brand-new team. I should note that this restaurant opening differed greatly from the previous one, mainly due to how my personal life had evolved over the years. Prior to this new restaurant opening, I had been house hunting and planning my wedding with my soon-to-be husband. A few days before the wedding, initial training at the restaurant had begun. So, I got married, enjoyed a quick two-day "clean up the wedding" honeymoon, and raced back to work. I was ready to tackle this next exciting adventure.

Immediately, I felt behind and overwhelmed by how much work I had to get caught up on. Contrary to last time, I now had a reason to go home and felt the pressure of balancing work and home life. And just as quickly, I felt I was failing at both. Each day I would struggle to decide which aspect of my life needed my attention. If I put the restaurant first, my home life would suffer. But if I wanted to make the restaurant a success, I needed to put in the time and effort! I couldn't win.

As the months progressed, I got deeper into the routine of putting work first. I would be gone for twelve to fourteen hours a day, my sleeping patterns and eating habits suffered, and my decisions revolved around work. Despite feeling exhausted, I would do my best to shake it off. I blared my pump-up playlist during my commute to remind myself of how fierce and determined I was. But even with that outstanding playlist, my mentality quickly went from "today will be better" to "just get through the shift." I would leave work feeling stressed and exhausted, and I would return home, reaching for alcohol to numb the feeling of defeat. With each late night, I would be faced with the concerned conversation from my husband of, "You need to slow down," or the blunter option of quitting my job. The conversations turned from supportive to frustrated. "He just doesn't get it," I told myself. The only way out of this situation was by accomplishing the goal that I set out to accomplish.

With each issue at work, I lost some belief in myself and my abilities. I kept giving it my best, yet somehow I was failing. Soon enough the stress caught up, and I started talking down to myself. I had created an island of self-pity in my mind and decided to isolate myself in that headspace. I hadn't called my parents in weeks. I didn't feel motivated or energetic enough to do anything on my days off. My personality was muted, and I genuinely had no care left for my own personal wellness. When I got home, one beer turned into two, which turned into however many I could get down before I fell asleep on the couch. Little did I realize, I had worked myself into a state of burnout. This was my lowest point. I had become so disconnected from myself that I was showing up as this zombie-like version of myself operating each day on autopilot. I had lost who I was. The worst part was that I couldn't even recognize what was happening to me.

A few months into this headspace, my parents invited me to join them on a trip to Mexico. Over the years, I had frequently chosen the business over my friends and family. In fact, I had perfected my rapid responses of: "There is no way that I could take that time off work." or "Who would cover for me while I was away?!" or "How on earth would they survive without me?"

Do any of those sound familiar to you? I had this impression that taking time off work showed weakness, incompetence, or even irresponsibility to my role and duties. All I knew was that I couldn't let anyone down! They were relying on me, and I had promised them I was the right woman for the job. But something inside me said, "You need to go on that trip."

To my surprise, I listened to that inner voice. I accepted the invitation to go to Mexico. Was it the right timing? Absolutely not! But at that moment, I decided I had to put myself first. I saw this trip as an opportunity for the downtime my body was craving. I needed space and time to look inward and a hug from my mother. So, I packed a bag, flew solo to Mexico, and met my parents at the resort.

This was a turning point for me. It was the first time that I put my personal life before my career. When I got to the resort, my parents were there greeting me with their typical embarrassing wave. This instantly made me smile. Suddenly, I felt like this vulnerable little girl that was just looking for a way to heal her pain. I grabbed hold of my parents and sobbed a mixture of happy and relieved tears. I finally felt the pressure I was experiencing melt away. Over the next few days, I spent time healing and reconnecting with myself and my parents. My afternoons involved laying by the pool reading a book, enjoying chicken wings and ice cream, taking in the breath-taking scenery and culture, chatting with my loved ones, and pampering myself with massages. For the first time in a while, I woke up each morning without an alarm, and without a hangover. I had set no expectations for myself other than to be present and grateful for this time. I could feel myself getting closer and closer to the person I once was. I finally allowed myself to let go of expectations and simply be present with myself.

One evening, we went out for a dinner excursion. On the boat ride over, the announcer mentioned a family of whales had been living in the area. As we docked, one worker came running over the edge of the boat and started shouting, "Whale, whale!"

I said a brief prayer asking some higher power to please let me see this whale. As I turned my head, this massive whale breached out of the water right next to our boat. I was in awe. In this moment, I felt a deep sense of comfort and peace. I felt a deep connection to the earth, to the world around me, to whatever higher power just heard my prayer, and most importantly, to my inner self. I stood there and continued to watch this whale joyfully swim and jump away into the distance. It was a moment I will never forget.

On my last day in Mexico, I was sitting alone on the beach as my parents caught an earlier flight home. As I stared out at the scenery, I saw the family of whales playfully jumping out of the water. Almost like it was planned, I watched my parents' flight take-off and fly right above me. Again came those tears. But this time, they were tears of happiness, love, and gratitude. I felt so grateful for this healing time with my parents. For the first time in a long time, I sat comfortably with myself and didn't feel totally lost or ashamed about who I was. This trip gave me a chance to breathe, to center myself, and to remember what was truly important to me. The next day, I returned home with a revitalized sense of self.

Three weeks after I returned home, the global pandemic temporarily shut down my restaurant and I was officially laid off from my career. At first, I panicked. Who am I if I'm not the general manager of a restaurant? That career title had been my identity for years. It was the reason I felt important, successful, and worthy of other people's admiration. Otherwise, I was just plain old Laura.

Within the first few days of the stay-at-home order, I tried to make myself as productive as possible and kept working towards some kind of personal growth. But as the weeks continued, I removed the pressure and expectations that I put on myself and allowed myself to just be present—like I was in that moment in Mexico. I allowed myself to catch up on sleep. I did some simple stretches in the morning and taught myself how to do wire-wrapped jewelry. I sat by the waterfront and enjoyed watching the waves roll in and the birds fly by. After a few weeks, I felt more curious, creative, and connected with "plain, old Laura." Feeling this new sense of inspiration, I completed the life coach certification that had been saved on my computer for months. As this time off continued, I began to appreciate and experience all the little things I had been missing out on over the years. I enjoyed dinners with my husband, zoom chats with my parents, and simply having time to sit and have my morning coffee. I had rediscovered my sense of self and purpose.

As I continued down this path of healing, I received confirmation from loved ones that they could see the changes I was experiencing. One night, my husband reiterated a comment made by my mother-in-law earlier that day: "I haven't heard Laura laugh like that in a long time."

This comment floored me. Finally, the pieces came together and something clicked. I hadn't been myself in so long. I took a moment and reflected on the past few years. Thoughts came flooding back to me about all those family trips that I gave up, or our wedding that I rushed through, or the extracurriculars that I stopped doing, all because I had to work. I thought about this version of myself that I created because I thought that "plain old Laura" wasn't good enough. "That's it," I thought to myself. I decided to change how I was living my life. I decided to see my worth as Laura, rather than my job title.

When my restaurant reopened, I noticed that I started moving further away from what was important to me and right back into my stress-filled routine. So, in July 2021, I made the difficult decision to leave my corporate career and pursue a new path. I struggled with this. In fact, I went back and forth on this decision for months, changing my mind every thirty seconds. I was struggling with the concept of leaving the amazing relationships I had built and the familiar role that I had become attached to. However, the biggest struggle for me was walking away from that unaccomplished goal. I thought I had failed.

On my last day at the restaurant, my team gave me a book that was filled with personalized goodbyes and farewell notes. Words and memories of respect, gratitude, and enlightenment filled the pages. Immediately I got emotional. I had been looking at success the wrong way for all these years! Success wasn't about the career title or the performance awards. To me, success was about the positive impact that I had on my team. Through these messages, I finally understood the pleas and concerned conversations from my husband and loved ones. All this time, they could see me for my value, my worth, and my inner light, even when I couldn't see it within myself. They knew I deserved more care and consideration than I was giving myself. Finally, I realized that "plain old Laura" was actually pretty amazing and deserved a lot more credit than I ever gave her. I finally felt at peace with my decision to leave my career.

Looking back, I could have walked away at any time and saved myself from this unpleasant experience. But no matter who tried to get through to me, something within me wouldn't walk away.

This wasn't about feeling pressure from my company or being encouraged that the show must go on. It was purely my pride getting in the way. I had put an insane amount of pressure on myself to be successful, perfect even, and it ultimately led me to my burnout experience. Over the years, I lost my sense of self. It took a full-blown global pandemic to make me slow down and reconnect with who I truly am. Take the time to slow down, reflect on how you're feeling, where you are in life, and do so respectfully and with love.

Chapter 11

Please, No Pictures

Christina Tam

"Have the courage to know yourself. It can create change that pays in dividends."

Christina Tam is a first-generation Canadian with two older sisters and a younger brother. Working in the telecommunications and insurance industries for more than fifteen years, she is a senior communications professional who counsels and writes for C-suite and senior executives. She also develops and implements communications strategies.

Christina's compelling moment came in 2016 when she realized she bore deep anger and sorrow stemming from her past. She sought support through therapy and continues to learn coping and forgiveness strategies. Christina's greatest lesson is understanding herself better; she's discovered reasons for her behaviors and reactions in the face of conflict and sadness. *Uncover Your Light* is her opportunity to share her story; she hopes it nudges others toward a quest to better understand and forgive themselves and others.

Christina is a self-proclaimed realist and accessories addict, who is morbidly and obsessively intrigued by true crime and all things horror, sci-fi, and Marvel.

fb: christinafacebooks ~ li: christinamtam

Put it all in a blender and set to 'on.'

Spotlight. Oh boy, does that word make me cringe—always has. Some things you just don't grow out of. As a kid, I remember feeling uneasy in situations in which I could be "inspected." I didn't enjoy taking photos, being on camera, or wearing dresses. Anything that would make me stand out was out of my comfort zone. So when teachers would proudly announce we were doing a class play or a group dance video for gym class, that was my cue to shrink like a violet. My parents and friends called out my timid and awkward behavior. In my report cards, some of my teachers wrote that I "should speak up if I had anything to say." And, as you read this, I'm doing just that.

On top of being the "oddball" and withdrawn, I didn't do a wonderful job of standing up for myself either; I was bullied by classmates, so-called friends, and eventually boyfriends. I wanted to blend in . . . and blend in, I did! That lovely place called "the background" was safe and comfortable. It still is.

I was a fixture in the backdrop of my family, too. From childhood into my adolescence, some family and "friends" often told me I had weight issues. Just a nice way of saying I was fat, really. The shaming continued at home. I was "too emotional," "too sensitive," and "abnormal." I struggled with my self-esteem as a result, which undoubtedly contributed to my shyness.

Having multiple siblings was a bit of a challenge for me. I didn't know my place or my own identity within my family and among my friends. I felt as though I didn't fit in anywhere. My eldest sister is, well, the oldest. She had her personal ways of getting attention from our parents. My second eldest sister was always more of an extrovert; independent, popular, and got involved in a ton of extracurricular activities. My brother is the youngest and a boy. If you know anything about Chinese culture, you know there's a lot of fanfare for baby boys. I remember my mom's friend was gifted a million dollars from her husband after giving birth to a boy, preceded by two daughters.

So, who was I? I didn't know. In the meantime, I fabricated some core beliefs and assigned myself the title of the "extra kid," the proverbial "middle child." In retrospect, I often felt ignored or unheard as a kid. When I tried to have conversations or build a relationship with my mom, I was dismissed on many occasions; I wasn't able to express myself and I never felt important or "normal." The outcome was a buzzing hypersensitivity to feeling unseen and, therefore, unsafe. I became triggered when ignored or unheard in my adult life, especially in relationships.

I attempted to gain attention from my parents by trying to be perfect. I regularly made the honor roll, did my homework before they asked me, and didn't procrastinate on any task. So, this shy perfectionist who didn't want attention wanted attention. Fucking paradox, right? Even if I got attention, I didn't believe I deserved it. It felt weird, and I'd quickly try to deflect the attention elsewhere. For the longest time, I couldn't even accept a compliment without grimacing. For better or worse, that was my identity. I internalized these traits and owned that narrative into my adulthood, along with the anxiety that developed as a by-product.

Annnd neat freak.

Since my sisters are five and ten years older than me, my brother and I, who are three years apart, spent a lot of time together. With my parents, I believed he could do no wrong, and attention was just given to him by virtue of being a boy. Although there were attempts to fade into the background, I subconsciously wanted attention from them, too. This manifested into me trying to be the "perfect child." It started suddenly, the memory so vivid as if it were yesterday. One day, I just started cleaning and organizing my bedroom. Everything went into the garbage. I had once kept or collected everything, even old chewing gum wrappers, then I kept nothing and became a minimalist overnight. Furniture was rearranged, drawers were cleaned out, belongings dusted, and things—I once thought were worth keeping—were purged. Nostalgia pretty much died that day, but it was therapeutic. From that point onward, I was a neat freak; I became obsessed with keeping things a particular way. Everything had its place. Decades later, I'd find out this was a coping mechanism for how I felt inside.

This obsessive-compulsive behavior didn't help my anxiety either, but top it off with some germaphobia and you have a cocktail of glamourous and unwavering pseudo-perfection that was chugged in regular quantities. Although, it came in pretty handy with the COVID-19 pandemic! There's always a silver lining.

My shiny new perfectionism also followed me into school. I got good grades and gave myself a hard time when I got an A instead of an A+. I started projects the day I received them and handed them in early. Being perfect bled into my social life, too. I stayed out of trouble for a long time. Typical teenage rites of passage, like trying alcohol or cigarettes, were beyond me, and so was self-compassion for mistakes I'd make along the way.

That ain't love, girl.

With friend groups, I blended in like a champ there as well. I wasn't the one in the limelight, didn't have the *cool clothes*, or have boys chasing me like my friends did. Guys would befriend me, confide in me, telling me how "cool" I was, while only speaking to me to get information on my "hot" friends. These disappointing experiences made me feel more like an observer than part of a group of friends. When I realized this in high school, I became a loner and found it tough to trust people. No identity, yet again.

Coupled with my blending-in superpower, I let people bully me. Constantly. All manner of so-called friends talked down to me and I believed everything they said: I was fat; I was nice, but not pretty; I only liked guys who didn't have standards on looks (yes, that's a real one). This all did a number on my already non-existent self-esteem. I even let someone I thought was a friend assault me as a teen. His reasoning? He "wanted to see how ruthless he could be."

Traits I used to define myself as a youngster followed me into my young adulthood. When it came to choosing romantic partners, the bullying theme played out there, too. I realize today that I chose men who kept me down in the mud. That's where I felt I belonged and they treated me like I deserved to be there. Ex-boyfriends put me down regularly, called me names, let their friends put me down, made fun of me, and laughed at my expense. I sought the wrong partners who'd tell me the same things I heard growing up, insulting my appearance and my weight, attacking my character. Acting overly accommodating and agreeable with no sense of self-worth in sight, I didn't stand up to them. Looking at my unhappiness through the tears, I saw someone I thought was weak, who abandoned herself to put the thoughts and wants of others before her own. After realizing this, I reached my emotional and verbal abuse thresholds pretty quickly and things didn't last because I no longer put up with their shit. Standing up for myself was a shock to them and additional name-calling and anger flew my way.

I remember one ex hid me from his family for the first three years of our relationship. The push-and-pull of wanting love and attention, and not getting it was so familiar from my upbringing, so I stayed for too long. Luckily, I realized it before walking down the aisle. With that ex, it took seven years for me to leave. With another, it took two years too long. This ex had a knack for cheating, so that was fun. Both were abusive in their own ways. I felt unworthy of love and went through many bouts of adjustment disorder. My self-worth dangled by a thin thread even after I left them. All of those life experiences make you feel you can't trust people, even though you so desperately want to. After all, decades of being pushed down again and again by people who are supposed to care about and love you takes its toll.

Pay no attention to that woman behind the curtain.

After double-majoring in Communications and French in university, I knew I wanted to use both assets in my career. By growing these interests and honing these skills, lo-and-behold, my chameleon-like ability followed me into the workplace. I chose a profession in (you guessed it) communications! Tasks like ghostwriting for executives, strategizing communications plans, and orchestrating events from behind the curtain, were and are thrilling to me. I found my niche.

Unsurprisingly, my perfectionism and lack of self-compassion came through at work as well. We all have learning opportunities, but if I got constructive feedback, didn't get that promotion by a certain time, or didn't make a specific salary by a particular age, I was downtrodden and beat myself up for it. If someone wasn't happy with my work performance, I'd fret and ruminate over it for days, weeks. Fundamentally, I knew perfectionism wasn't achievable, but it didn't stop me from trying.

Shots fired on Everest.

I had and still have a lot of climbing to do to overcome many of those mountainous obstacles from my past—my personal Mount Everest. Although often stigmatized, I strongly believe every one of us could use guidance from a mental health professional at one point or another. And if someone judges or shames you for needing support, that's a reflection of them, not you. Life isn't perfect and dealing with the shit life throws at us doesn't have to be done alone. Personally speaking, therapy is a blessing. It takes courage to climb and get over life's valleys, to be a better person, know yourself better, and have the willingness and bravery to pursue personal growth. Everybody has something. An experience. A childhood. A story. Self-awareness is the first step to self-repair.

As humans, we have an innate desire to feel heard, loved, understood, and safe. That's our MO, like it or not. You see it at work, home, school . . . I'm that textbook case study of a person who didn't process childhood trauma, like bullying, neglect, and emotional and verbal abuse. The unproductive result was reacting in not-so-admirable ways as an adult when I felt unsafe, unloved, unheard, and misunderstood. Given that we humans love to remain in our comfort zones, no matter how toxic they are, we generally choose partners who feel familiar to us. Well shit, no wonder why I dated the men I did. These guys offered me exactly what I was already accustomed to growing up: feeling ignored, dismissed, and insulted, intermingled with that tug-o-war of feeling loved and unloved. These ingredients cooked up a pretty crappy level of self-esteem, some heavy triggers, and the pinnacle of resentment, defensiveness, and maladaptive coping skills.

Of course, I wouldn't have even known all of this amazing goodness had it not been for that magical "T" word called therapy.

I'd sought professional guidance in the past, but it never seemed to quite work out. I'd see a therapist for a few sessions, then fall off the therapy wagon. Finding the right connection with a therapist is like finding the right fit for a stubborn puzzle piece: it isn't always easy, but it's completely worth it when you place it where it belongs. And alas, the puzzle feels a bit more complete. After years of work, I found that identity I wanted so badly when I was a kid.

The above lessons are just some of the healing and remarkable realizations I'm fortunate enough to have uncovered. Those moments of discovery hit me so hard, it was probably like being shot . . . minus the violence . . . and blood. Being able to understand why you get triggered or why you think the way you do in specific situations, like in relationships, is so insanely satisfying. Maybe you've heard of attachment theory? Learning about it can be an eye-opening experience, helping you understand why you react the way you do in the face of relationship conflict, romantic or not. Simply put, your attachment style is formed through your relationships with your primary caregivers, usually your parents. It's your learned understanding of love and intimacy, stemming from what we were modeled during our developmental years. When we become adults, the role of "primary caregiver" usually transfers to our romantic partner. So if your parents neglected you emotionally or were consistently absent when you needed them, you might develop low self-worth; you might also feel unsafe expressing emotion or getting close to anyone because you were taught you couldn't rely on anyone. This is called an avoidant attachment style. As effed up as it sounds, we usually pick partners who feel familiar, which occurs at a subconscious level. If you had a tumultuous relationship with your mom or pops, you may end up with someone with whom you have a similarly unstable relationship.

Self-compassion was also another powerful lesson. Perfection isn't realistic, nor is it achievable. Writing out affirmations is one exercise I've found helpful in adjusting this thinking and lowering anxiety related to the high expectations you may set for yourself. These sentences describe who you strive to be in the present tense, and reading them regularly actually fucking works, believe it or not! One of my affirmations is that I won't put up with being dismissed or ignored—a boundary I created for myself. Despite all the gaslighting in the world, these are legitimate feelings and this affirmation helps stop me from abandoning my needs for those of another person.

Therapy also offers me new coping skills, and healthier conflict management and communication strategies. I learned what triggers my partner and managed to shift the dynamic in my relationship. Each therapy session is valuable because I continually learn about myself, heal old wounds; and most importantly, identify the many harsh words and people I still need to forgive to finally feel free.

Mirror, mirror . . .

I now know, after working through those realizations and gaining an understanding of my upbringing, that it wasn't my parents' fault. They taught me and modeled what they knew, what they were shown, so how could I fault them for that? It doesn't mean there isn't some residual hurt; it just means accepting and processing my way through it. Although it may take a lifetime to undo decades of repressed pain and reach the summit, I know I am and will be a happier and better person for it.

Today, I embrace my awkwardness, my sensitivity, and my introversion. My arms are wide open to my identity as one of four siblings who has her own personality, quirks, and sense of humor. Thankfully, I experience growth through therapy and, while nothing worth having comes easy, it's worth it to turn around, honor and love thyself, and look in the mirror.

Chapter 12

Be the Light

Sandra Blais

"Everyone has the power to change their lives, on occasion we need someone further down the path to guide our way."

Sandra was born and raised in Alberta, Canada, and currently resides in the greater Edmonton area. Sandra received her Bachelor of Applied Science in Environmental Management and since then her career has seen her serve as a public servant. Further to this, Sandra is very passionate about choice, both personally and financially, and has invested much time in the pursuit of becoming an entrepreneur. Sandra considers her family and the pursuit of helping others to be part of her core values. If she isn't spending time with her husband or son, you can almost always find her buried in a book, whether that is for self-improvement, leadership development, financial literacy, or a fun mythical fantasy! This is Sandra's first endeavor as a co-author.

ig: sandy321ca ~ fb: Sandra Daisy Blais

Is This It?

I had just moved into our new custom-built house, had an established career, a wonderful marriage, and a beautiful, healthy baby boy. From the outside looking in, my husband Westin and I had a life that most people strive for. I should've been grateful and happy, but something wasn't sitting right. I was just existing, repeating the same day.

I had reached the point where I was struggling with who I thought I should be versus who I wanted to be. The problem: I didn't know what that looked like, nor did I know anyone that was thriving in life. I couldn't put my finger on it, just a gnawing, hollowness growing inside me. When I shared how I felt with Westin, I discovered he also believed there must be more to life.

I was torn between what my life was and what I envisioned my life to be. I always wanted to make a difference, have adventures, create experiences, and help people. I thought my life would be a grand adventure filled with amazing intrigues and traveling the world. I didn't know how to get from where I was to where I wanted to be. Thankfully, Westin had the same vision, and we began to figure out what we wanted our life to look like. We started exploring how to change our lives. What we didn't realize at the time was that "how?" was the wrong question. What we should've been asking was "who?".

First the "why": we determined our vision was choice. We wanted to have the freedom to choose who we spent time with, where and how to travel, what charities and causes to support, and how to provide for our parents. I wanted to live comfortably and have a sense of peace. We had to decide if we were willing to change to reach our vision.

At the time, I still enjoyed my job, so Westin quit. This was not an easy decision but was the best for our family. The atmosphere change in our house was astronomical. A positive energy and a sense of peace filled our home. We pulled Ethan from the day home and Westin was able to be a full-time dad, which he loved. We also recognized that we needed to bring in additional income and the obvious choice was real estate. We already had rentals, so expansion seemed like the logical next step.

As we were expanding our real estate portfolio, I started climbing the corporate ladder. That involved working more hours, being away from home more often, and missing precious moments of my son's life. The gnawing feeling came back and started growing.

We started buying, renovating, and suiting rental properties. It was the worst financial decision we've ever made. I cannot even begin to convey the shame, guilt, and embarrassment I felt by putting my family in such a dire financial situation. Going all in without the proper training and information. Taking poor advice because we didn't know how to evaluate the source of the advice. Plowing ahead, using other people's money, and eventually maxing out all our credit options. We desperately wanted it to work and felt like we had no control over our future. The weight of this was indescribable and the frustration level: epic. We were ignoring that real estate was not giving us the results we were looking for until we couldn't ignore it anymore. We had to take a step back from the emotional and time commitment and evaluate the results of our efforts. After eight years, we decided it was time to exit and divest from real estate.

Despite the hardships, this experience cemented the vision we wanted for our lives—we wanted choice. Choice meant control of our time, finances, and mental energy. We wanted to help others who were looking to find the same. Our first step was to become debt-free.

This meant no more vacations, going out less, and learning how to discipline ourselves. Most importantly, we learned how to switch our mindset from spending money to investing money. Essentially, we had to dramatically change our life so we could grow in the future.

I lacked self-awareness. It wasn't until my thirties that a wonderful woman, Sasha, came into my life and was courageous enough to point some things out. To this day, she is one of my best friends.

Sasha helped me start my growth journey and sparked my interest in taking control of my life and my personal development. Sometimes, I struggle to understand people. I am hard to offend and have good control of my emotions. That led to people thinking I was cold and had no feelings. I didn't back down from a debate and I came across as challenging instead of genuinely seeking to understand. Because of help from Sasha, I realized how I was coming across, in most cases, did not reflect that intent.

I was made fun of—a lot. I was bullied, talked about, undermined, criticized, and continuously "put in my place." I faced most of it with a smile and saved my tears for when I was alone. Frankly, I wasn't mentally equipped to understand why this was happening. Clarity on these situations came much later.

As I became more self-aware, I went into a negative headspace that spiraled. As memories of confusing or bad experiences surfaced, I started seeing clearly how my actions created those negative situations. I would never intentionally hurt or belittle someone, yet that's how I came across. That realization hit me like a brick wall and I decided to change. I fumbled and stumbled, but I started. Reading, networking, TedTalks, and Google were the first step on this new adventure. Gradually, I increased my self-awareness and equipped myself with tools to help me communicate more effectively.

My next big "aha" moment was during mandatory leadership training through work. I'd completed my first personality test and, through a round of other tests and challenges, the instructor tapped me on the shoulder and asked me to stay after class. She asked if I'd ever felt like I was alone on an island. My response was: "all the time!"

She explained that the way I perceive and see things is uncommon. She equipped me with tools and strategies to recognize and improve my communication with others. Intense relief flooded over me. For so long, I'd felt like I was missing something and didn't belong. Instead, I needed to prepare myself properly, analyze the way I saw things, and then apply the appropriate tools and systems.

At this point, I started evaluating everything in my life and asking myself an amazingly simple question: "Is this getting me closer to my vision?" If the answer was no, I limited my exposure or cut it out of my life. I evaluated my daily habits, my associations, my relationships, and my budget. I didn't want to be stagnant in my life and couldn't put my finger on what I wanted. I recognized that four things had to change in my life if I wanted different results:

Associations

Money management

Mindset

Action

Our associations determine where we end up in life. I needed to find people who were living the way I wanted to and find out how they did it. I had mentors at work, maybe I needed one for my life. As we change the way we look at things, things around us start to change . . . enter Carly.

Carly forever changed my life because she had the courage to share her experience with me. She had recently earned mentorship and explained to me how this was already having a positive influence in her life. I immediately asked if her mentor, Anita, was looking to take on new mentees. Carly didn't promise anything but was able to make an introduction. On the day of our meeting, I sat nervously at a coffee shop when the most beautiful woman I'd ever seen swept in. A light radiated from her that immediately caught my attention. I thought, "I want to know whatever this woman knows."

That was the beginning of one of the most important relationships in my life. Anita and her husband Oliver took me and Westin under their wings. They taught us the importance of critical thinking and to question why we think the way we do. For the first time, I questioned why I had the limiting beliefs that I had. I asked myself where they stemmed from and whether or not they were true. They taught us how to think, not what to think. If we could learn to think critically and evaluate the way we make decisions, we could achieve different results. It opened a whole new world to us.

This relationship has forever changed the trajectory of our lives. Anita and Oliver helped us focus on the kind of life we wanted to live instead of what we wanted to be when we grew up. Most importantly, they provided us a safe place, free of judgment to seek perspective and advice based on actual experience and results. We now pay that forward.

I was good at making decisions and making good decisions—except where I was at in my life was not what I wanted it to be. Then, a realization hit me: I hadn't planned for it to look any different. I, like most people I know, spend more time planning a weeklong vacation than planning my life. Upon reflection, I had an epiphany. I was a reactive decision-maker who allowed circumstances to dictate where my life headed. I was like a dinghy in the ocean, going wherever the waves took me. To be clear, I still made these decisions for my life, I just did not have an overall plan of what I wanted my life to look like to guide these decisions. I needed a north star, a vision for my life, so I could start making proactive decisions every day.

I couldn't do that while I didn't have control of my time and money. The joy and gratitude that I have for meeting the love of my life at twenty-five and the beauty of our son is tremendous. It's because of these events that I wanted more from life and more for their lives. I didn't want to rely on a job for my financial freedom. Being able to make my decisions based on my values, not the amount in my bank account. Create experiences and memories. We wanted choice in our life . . . but how? Then we discovered that was the wrong question, the right question was: who?

Allowing Anita and Oliver to speak into our lives changed everything. The best decisions my mind could make led me to exactly where I was. I sought their perspective and knowledge, then applied it to my life so that I could change the results I was getting. And we are privileged to pay it forward. The more we help others get what they want in life, the more we will get in ours.

I had to change my mindset from scarcity to abundance. I equipped myself with the knowledge of how to think instead of what to think. I built a cash-flowing asset while learning how to appropriately invest my money and time. When I surrounded myself with people who wanted more, I also became one of the dreamers and the doers.

I've learned amazing lessons that no one ever shared with me, but here are a few that I believe are the keys to success in life:

Change is a choice. You can choose to change everything. It

may suck and be the most difficult thing you've ever done, but it's worth it.

It's all about mindset.

I have control over the way I think, feel, and act.

When I take my eyes off myself, I help others achieve what they are looking to achieve.

A title at a job or level of education doesn't define who you are as a person, nor does it set the limitations of what you can achieve.

Simple does not mean easy.

It is not what you know but who you know. Association will make or break you.

Change the question from "What do you want to do?" to "What kind of life do you want to live?"

Love people but have boundaries. People will treat you the way you allow them to treat you.

If I could put this much effort into a job, what could my life look like if I put this much effort into it?

Stop blaming everyone else for your situation.

When taking advice or listening to someone else's opinion, ask yourself, "Does this person have the life I want to live?" If the answer is no, then don't take the advice or listen to their opinion, even if they love you.

Remember, "It ain't what you don't know that gets you into trouble. It's what you know for sure that just ain't so." - Mark Twain

The changes I have made in my life are based on the following:

I have switched my mindset from short-term thinking to long-term planning.

Taking control of my finances and eliminating excuses.

Discipline and consistency.

Tweaking, not overhauling, and getting 1% better every day.

Learning how to invest my time and invest my money, not waste my time and spend my money.

Unlearn, relearn then apply.

It's all about mindset.

Find someone who is living the life you want and then get them to show you how. There are lots of people with money and no time, and lots of people with time and no money. Stop letting what you do for a living define who you are as a person. Get uncomfortable, unlearn, learn, and apply. It is the results that matter, not the title or position we hold.

Is this it? Absolutely not, it's just the beginning. We can change, we can hope, and we can help others along the way.

Chapter 13

Courage to Create Connections

Rupinder Sidhu

"Let the light of kindness shine through infinitely."

Rupinder Sidhu is a daughter, sister, wife, and mother, whose sole purpose is to help those around her with their journeys. Rupinder has been a veteran elementary school multicultural worker for over thirty-two years. Not only is she a leader in creating school-wide workshops, but she has also worked with many students with various needs. Her passion lies in helping families build confidence in the school system and teaching them how to advocate for their children, furthering connections around care and kindness.

In all areas of life, Rupinder enjoys connecting with and empowering her circle. This includes entertaining and creating a home where everyone is welcome and feels like they can just drop by and stay for a bit—or a while. Kind-hearted, grateful, thoughtful, and brave are just a few of the words that her loved ones use to describe her.

When taking time for herself, Rupinder is a foodie. She enjoys cooking, going for ice cream, and having meaningful conversations over a cup of coffee. She also loves being in nature, reading, and anything Zen. Above all else, her priority remains to lend a helping hand when able, spreading kindness and warmth, and creating a caring space for everyone.

ig: rupesidhu69 ~ fb: rupinder.sidhu.963

I was just a young child walking to school. All I had to do was go up the little hill, turn left, and down the road. It was a busy road with cars swishing by. A little scary, but all I had to do was press the button for the crosswalk and look both ways before I crossed. So I looked both ways and waited for the green light to come on. As I walked along watching cars go by, I got hit by something on my arm. I was startled by the voices saying, "Go back to your country you Hindu! You stink! Look at her clothes."

I wondered why they were saying such horrible things to me. I was born here. Why did they throw things at me? Confused, I ran to school. The next day, I was afraid of walking to school by myself, but I didn't want to tell my parents, so I walked hesitantly, watching all around me, hoping and praying it wouldn't happen again.

I feared that people who were not the same color as me would say something to make me feel hurt or embarrassed about being a different color. As I grew up and went to high school, the taunting continued. I got harassed as I walked to school. It was a long thirty-minute walk. A particular group of boys kept saying I smelled like curry. "Hey, let me play with those long braids . . . we could jump rope with them. You probably can't even understand English," they spat at me.

It went on for six months before I decided enough was enough: "I am going to stand up for myself," I said.

I scared them off, but they spread rumors at the school. "She's crazy—watch out, she might go berserk and come after you!"

After going through the challenges in my elementary and high school years, I knew I wanted to help people who were being treated unfairly. I wanted to spread kindness, regardless of where anyone came from. It was important for me to communicate with others around me and make everyone feel welcome.

The women in my family have been the biggest support in my life. From them, I have learned to be resilient and brave, yet warm and nurturing. My maternal grandmother lived by herself in a small village in Punjab. She raised her four children while her husband immigrated to Canada to find a better life for them. My paternal grandmother persevered through life after losing her husband and immigrating to Canada. My mother has passed her warmth and quiet strength on to her five daughters. She reminds us to always give 110 percent to everything we do and help others as much as we can. All these strong-minded and passionate women endured so many hardships, yet they thrived and taught the next generations to work hard, be honest, be caring, and be there for others—all while building a prosperous life for their families. The strength to carry on in difficult times has been passed on to all of the women in my family. As I look around, I see that resolve to elevate everyone around us in our unique ways. So many of the women in my family have taken on professions that help others flourish. I am proud to be a part of that circle of powerful lionesses.

Even before I was a multicultural worker, I just wanted people to know how it feels to be treated differently when all you want to do is feel a sense of belonging. It is so motivating to watch the students' faces light up while we do cultural celebrations and when they see that their culture is being recognized. Everyone feels so much pride when they can share information about things they learned at home. I can't believe it has been over thirty-two years of helping families in the community that I love to work in. We all want to be accepted, loved, and seen. It doesn't matter *what* we celebrate but that we *all* celebrate by having good food, dressing up, and sharing that moment with friends and family. What we do for our community matters.

My motivation of wanting to help others started with helping some cousins learn English. When they arrived from India I realized the way to help them learn English was by watching TV and giving them examples of the vocabulary they would need to communicate in different situations. It felt so empowering to watch them become more fluent and independent. They taught me that it only takes a little patience to help others grow.

From there I became an education assistant and loved working with new immigrants to help them learn the language. We learned about the nuances, how to adapt to the environment, and how to understand the cultural norms and celebrations through experiences. We facilitated these lessons through cooking, playing games, and doing field trips while learning English. Discovering that learning the language was quicker with actual life experiences rather than looking at pictures because students were more engaged. Costumes, and people knocking at your door dressed up in them, can be scary for someone from a different country who hasn't celebrated Halloween. We made sure new immigrant families understood what happened during that time.

Smiling at everyone lets people know it is safe to approach you for help. It's important to observe and read body language to see if others around you are comfortable. Ask your neighbor about what is celebrated in their home. Learn simple words and sentences in different languages. Share the significance of different clothing and talk about when they are worn.

Twelve years later, I became a multicultural worker. I love connecting with families, listening to their needs, and then bridging them with our schools. How can we create classroom lessons that encompass all cultures and celebrate everyone? How can we help a grandparent who doesn't know where to pick up their grandchild but doesn't know how to ask for directions? We need to bridge that language barrier. We can comfort others by being calm and understanding when they are fearful of new surroundings. Connecting two parents who speak the same language, or are familiar with the same culture, helps those with no other family or friends in Canada. Even a small action, such as helping a new family buy basic supplies because they don't know where to get these items, is incredibly helpful. Consider how the exchange of ideas can make another person feel comfortable when they are new to an environment. *Listen* to their story and assume nothing.

Learning the correct pronunciation of names also helps build a connection. It pays respect to their identity and creates an atmosphere of understanding, kindness, and compassion. That is why I always ask any new family starting at our school for the correct pronunciation of the student's name. Sometimes we find that the child will not respond to the teacher if the name is being mispronounced.

Let's learn together and lead with our hearts!

Earlier on in my journey, I found it was really difficult to keep hearing things like: "Why don't these parents look at us when we talk to them? Why don't they learn English? Why do they keep nodding their heads in a figure eight?" At this time, we decided to offer cultural nuance workshops for staff so they could learn that some of the things that others thought were disrespectful here were actually a sign of respect where they came from. It's important to create great connections, accept everyone for who they are, and learn the different needs of each family. I also always try to remember not to assume anyone needs help because if you are second, third, or fourth-generation Canadian or if you know English then there is no need for assistance. I find that introducing myself in English and then asking if they prefer to speak in English or a different language isn't disrespectful to families. We give information on school programs, interpret report cards, offer notices on school holidays, field trips, hot lunches, and parent-teacher interviews so the families that need the interpretation feel comfortable to ask questions. There is no time limit—it is a life-long journey, slow and steady.

Never stop trying and never doubt your worth. *You are worthy*! I've had to navigate a lifetime of figuring out who I am, two different cultural values, gender inequality, racism, not fitting the mold, and losing opportunities because I was seen as "different." My dad used to tell me that you have to have confidence and be fearless. Don't let anyone tell you what you should wear or what you should look like. Do what feels right for you. He always taught us to be honest and help others whenever we could. Dad was always told by others that he needed a son. When I heard this I decided at a very young age that I needed to be better than any son. So I have spent my life doing just that and trying to empower other girls. Reach for the stars and break the glass ceilings. Given a chance women can accomplish anything they want. This is also why I learned to be independent and not rely on anyone but myself. Before my dad passed away from cancer, he said he was so proud to have all his girls and he was so lucky to have each of us there helping him and taking care of him with mom. That helped my soul heal.

Listen from the heart. I am humbled when a parent or grandparent shares their struggles with me. I try my best to help them resolve the situation. Sometimes giving them a warm smile and a tissue is all they need to feel seen. It is uplifting for me when a parent asks if I have a brother or a son and I say no to both. I love explaining how I am the oldest of five daughters and have one daughter myself; how I am grateful to be where I am in life and can share my positive experiences with them also empowering them. Other times I enjoy sharing food and a cup of chai with a parent that has helped me run an all-day school event; when I see the parents smile because we are celebrating their culture; when I can appreciate them by offering them a flower for volunteering even though I know they are not comfortable speaking English.

Everyone needs to be who they truly are and receive love for who they are, without judgment. Look past the color, gender, race, age, status, and diversity of any kind. It takes courage to do this, but we are all capable if we try.

One day a child came up to me crying because someone had told them to go back to where they came from even though they were Canadian by birth. I asked the teacher if we could talk to the class about how we may all look different but we all have the same feelings and we all want to be cared for, acknowledged, and to feel like we belong here. How are we going to use our courage to roar against racism, unfairness, and bullying? Be a friend to the new person in our class, workplace, or neighborhood. Share a smile with them! We don't develop resilience by always having it easy; we get it from going through tough times and getting through them together. Treat others as we would want to be treated. Strength comes from within sometimes—just when we think there is nothing more to give, we find a way to shine more light. Look inside for that change and then *be* the change!

The hardships that I faced as a child molded me to be who I am today. When people said things that hurt my feelings, I chose to be calm. I let them know how their actions impacted me. Then I led by example. Just because someone smiles doesn't mean that they are not scared or not worried. When a student or parent looks like they are confused, ask them how they are doing. Ask: "Is there anything

I can do to clarify things?" Do we walk by or do we take that minute to stop? More and more, I feel that all the trials of life make us stronger, braver, more helpful, more kind, caring, and empathetic. We are meant to be lifelong learners.

Creating and sharing experiences without fear of judgment is necessary for our authentic selves to shine. I have had the privilege of creating trust with the families I have worked with, which has helped create pathways to engage more openly with newcomers in my community. I believe it will help all those around me. So, let's create connections to heal.

How do we spread light? I choose courage, compassion, and kindness to turn ignorance into love. I am so grateful for each parent that takes the time to come and chat with me or call me when they don't understand something. I have the privilege of learning new ways to support the families that I work with every day. By respecting each other and connecting at a level that both sides are comfortable with, we can solve problems. Give from your whole heart—not just because it is a formality or obligation, but because you truly want to help and make this a better world for everyone around you. I do this by asking myself what I can do to make these school years better for the families that I work with; connecting families to other resources that they may not know of; having honest conversations when things are not working out; finding solutions for those problems together. Let's help each other become better versions of ourselves by having those courageous conversations to understand and respect each other. We need to cultivate meaningful connections with each other. So many amazing people in my life have taught me that simplicity and kindness are all that I need to be at peace with who I am. This is what I think will create a world filled with light and acceptance.

Regardless of whether someone agrees or disagrees with a person's cultural background, norms, or experiences, all people should be treated with respect, compassion, and kindness. Let's help each other uncover the light within ourselves. As the saying goes, "You can't understand someone until you've walked a mile in their shoes."

Chapter 14

Becoming Desirable

Eva Wong

"I didn't start taking care of myself and my appearance so I could love myself. It's quite the opposite. I love myself so I started taking care of myself inside and out."

Eva Wong is an adventurous soul with a curious mind. She enjoys exploring the endless wonders of nature and learning about the history and culture of different places. Being raised in the South Pacific to Chinese parents exposed her to multiple cultures living harmoniously with the islands. She spent most of her childhood with her grandmother, who used storytelling to share family history and stories of her ancestors. After graduating from the International Studies Program at the University of Oregon, Eva returned home to Fiji to help her parents for a couple of years before going to Beijing for Chinese Language Studies on a scholarship. Living in Beijing enriched her understanding of Chinese culture and history. After that, she lived in Toronto and California before moving to Ottawa, where she spent years raising her children before her midlife awakening. Her passion for art reignited as she began her journey of becoming a professional photographer. Her mission was to empower women by capturing their unique beauty. Meanwhile, she discovered her new love for writing and comedy amid life's turmoil. Her new mission is to empower others with her stories and sprinkle some sparkles in their lives.

evawong.photography

ig: evawong.photography ~ fb: evawong.photography

In 2015, all I could think of was becoming a professional photographer. I had been a photographer since the age of eleven, the day my dad gave me a camera as my consolation prize. He had refused to buy me any more art supplies. It was his attempt to remove any resources I could use to become an artist in the future. At thirty-seven, I decided to become a professional photographer. My true love was boudoir photography because it could empower women by allowing them to see how beautiful they are through my lenses.

One client, who was a prettier version of Meg Ryan, walked into my life and I was so excited to help her document this major milestone of hers. She was healing from a recent separation, and although she was turning fifty, she looked nothing over thirty-seven. My favorite part of the entire process was the conversation with "Meg Ryan" as she was getting her hair and make-up done in the studio. "Meg" shared her struggles with me about her body image and that she'd had eating disorders for many years. Not only was she gorgeous, but she was also in great shape. She was a fitness coach who had the body and fitness level of women in their twenties. Yet, here she was, struggling to find beauty in herself. I wanted to snap her out of it without undermining her struggles, but I soon heard the things I said about myself: "I need a tummy tuck."

We went back and forth, reassuring each other that we were beautiful and perfect the way we were. The boudoir session was so much fun and "Meg" was as stunning in person as she was in the photos.

However, that night, I questioned my ability to empower women. How could I help them see how beautiful and desirable they are when I still struggle with the same negative self-talk? I felt tired, fat, and undesirable. I didn't spend time looking in the mirror because I had become a stranger to my reflection when my first child was born. I felt like a fraud as a boudoir photographer, so

I dug deeper and searched for the beauty in me. It took me back to my childhood in Fiji.

My mother's voice still lived in my head, reminding me how I was always too tanned, too muscular, or too tall for a girl. I paid little attention to nor acknowledged her whenever she decided to insult me, but her words set a guideline for what the standards of beauty were for a Chinese girl. So, I accepted that I wasn't beautiful. At times, I felt sorry for my poor mother who got so worked up over the fact that I would come home two shades darker than when I left that morning. My dog didn't seem to care. She loved me just the same without barking about my unappealing appearance.

It was difficult to comprehend why my mom was so persistent in fitting me into her standards. She already had my sister whom everyone praised for her fair complexion, oval face, and petite stature. All I cared about was that our school's netball team wouldn't come last in the open district competition. I learned about failure and disappointment rather early in life when our school didn't make it to the quarterfinals. The school was known for its academics, and its rapport in sports was close to non-existent. I was a disappointment to my parents because I was a tomboy who was quick to speak my mind.

Entering high school, I finally gave in to my mom's daily complaints and nagging. I stopped playing sports and that side of myself became a well-kept secret. Each day I would massage my face, trying to slim down my round cheeks until the sides of my face bruised. In 1993, my parents decided to send me and my siblings to the United States to finish high school. After the first two years of living in Eugene, Oregon, I successfully super-sized myself with fast food and late-night ice cream runs. The extra fifty pounds was an expensive, non-surgical enhancement that required a lot of bad eating and couch-potatoing. I assure you, gaining so much weight wasn't something one could achieve overnight. It took two years of stagnation and junk food consumption to get there with much unintended dedication.

When I returned home in 1994 for our visit, my then-boyfriend couldn't even recognize me. Partially because my mom made me perm my hair, which turned out to be a disaster. I looked like an

Asian aunty with a 'fro. When I was chubby with the extra weight, I felt like the Pillsbury Doughboy, but now I was more like the Michelin Tire Man with an aunty fro. My self-esteem shattered right before me as he walked right past me on the street.

During my senior year of high school, I was lucky enough to have someone ask me out to prom. It was unexpected. I remember I was stinking with sweat masked by the smell of heavy hairspray. I was dying for air in my body-shaper. That was even before Spanx was invented. I felt like I looked like a Hawaiian dude in a dress standing next to him.

During university, I was living in a townhouse with my siblings and cousin. Our place seemed to be the hub for all of our friends. One day, a Victoria's Secret catalog arrived in the mail and was left on the kitchen counter. As soon as the guys came in, they started fighting for the catalog. This was still before the days of Google or online catalogs. I was curious about what the fuss was all about, so I got in there with the boys. As they flipped through the pages, they talked about who was their favorite model and to my surprise, Tyra Banks was their "it" girl. In my mind, I was like, "As if you could please her. You wouldn't even know what to do if she was naked right in front of you." I agree Tyra was drop-dead gorgeous with a tanned complexion and curves in all the right places. My question was, "Don't all Asian guys like fair complexions and petite girls?" Tyra was not petite in the Asian definition.

Months later, my cousin's surprise birthday present from me finally arrived in the mail. It was a subscription to *Playboy Magazine*. He was really shy about it and hardly looked at it. I actually got it for him as a present but realized the present was more for my amusement than his. As expected, our guy friends took no time to go through them. Again, I was curious to see what they would consider desirable and attractive in women. Most of the Playboy models had very similar body structures and, at that time, there was very little ethnic representation. The concept of attractiveness and sexiness were visually fed to our population through media. The 36D, 24, 36/38 figure was considered the ideal sexy female figure. Who can compare to that? It wouldn't matter because as women, we still try to.

Being a size eleven for the six crucial years of my life was an emotional struggle. From eating a mountain of junk food to starving myself, I just wasn't losing any weight. Starving myself didn't help, because my body retained every calorie I was consuming. Towards the end of 1999, I purchased a book from a catalog about the five secrets of weight loss. It changed my life. I learned to eat a balanced diet and became active again. It took over two months to feel better and close to six months to lose a couple of pounds. After eighteen months, I lost my first twenty pounds. I started to look good in some clothes again. Three years later, I was almost back to looking like myself, but it did not make me feel more confident as a person. I still felt overweight, unattractive, and not good enough. My inner identity remained to be this unattractive chubby girl who was more like a Hawaiian dude. I had finally asserted my mom's voice and developed a self-shaming mindset. I rejected compliments because I became comfortable knowing that I was not pretty or good enough.

By the time I was twenty-five years old, I second-guessed all my decisions. I used to quit before I started and always chose the easier route. Moreover, I had a track record of dating grandiose narcissists and losers. I didn't feel good enough for anyone decent, nor did I know what a decent guy should be like. My bar for dating was so low. I ended up marrying a covert narcissist who wanted me to be his "domestic servant." He expected me to give up my dreams, my needs, and myself so I could serve his needs and support his dreams. I simply didn't think I deserved love.

Two children and three years later, I finally felt that I had earned the right to reach for my dreams and work on becoming a photographer. At thirty-eight, a year after "Meg" came into my life to remind me of my need for a self-love check-in, I took a good look in the mirror and was shocked to see my face, like I was a stranger to myself. I couldn't remember how I used to look and I also couldn't recognize the person in the reflection. I said to myself, "Girl, you better put on some make-up. It is your civic duty to make sure you don't scare anyone to death." Slowly, I reacquainted myself with the stranger in the mirror by putting on eyeliner, mascara, and tons of concealer on her eye bags. Some days I would even tell her she looked sort of human again. "Next challenge, buy yourself some decent clothes that don't look like cheap t-shirts."

After my third child was born, I had mastered the art of hiding my flabby tummy. My kids would ask me why my belly was so jiggly, and I would show them my "belly dancing move" just to make them laugh. I told them I had been stretched three times and earned this belly flap so I could become a jiggly belly dancer. Of course, it was a joke. A part of me refused to talk down to myself in front of my kids because I didn't want to project my self-esteem issues onto them. Another part of me really didn't care so much anymore. That was a strange feeling. Did I let myself go? Or did I get rid of that undesirable, self-shaming, inner Hawaiian dude? As a mother, I must be a good example to my kids to help them develop healthy self-worth, and as a boudoir photographer, I must be able to see my beauty and embrace my flaws in order to empower the women whom I might be so lucky to cross paths with.

It was an eye-opener to take that journey and discover what kept me from feeling desirable as a person. I am a funny, kind, and smart person with an open mind. I have many beautiful qualities inside but I never felt that they would count for much more than a nicely layered sandwich with ugly bread. The first thing you see repels you from wanting to see what is inside. A walk through my past made me realize that I needed to unlearn things so I could clear out the voices that repeatedly played in my head. I didn't go through some soul-cleansing boot camp or Tony Robbins workshops. I joined Toastmasters to practice my public speaking so I could be more confident with business networking and eventually give stand-up comedy a try. I started delivering speeches. I was writing my stories and listening to them as I presented them. I started acknowledging my voice and slowly began to trust my feelings and judgment. In addition, I started journaling, listening to music, and reading self-improvement books. I spilled my anger and frustrations onto the pages. It suddenly dawned on me that how I felt about myself had directly affected the way I made my life choices. I had second-guessed my decisions every time with my parents' voices playing in the background, "Being a photographer is not a real job! We spent so much money on your education! You must be the reason for the break-up of your marriage because you are too much of a princess! You dress like a beggar! All your clothes are so ugly and unpresentable!"

Little by little, I unlearned the ideals and traditional perception of what makes a person beautiful and desirable. Most of all, I stopped holding myself up against the standard of beauty put out by my mother and the companies who were trying to sell lingerie and sex appeal.

I started to feel comfortable with myself and embraced the little freckles, the little lines from years of smiling, and the scars on my forehead with stories behind them.

Now, in my forties, I finally learned to love myself. I put a little bit of care and effort into the way I dress, do my hair and make-up while eating healthy, and making time to exercise. Don't get me wrong, I didn't start taking care of myself and my appearance so I could love myself. It's quite the opposite! I love myself so I started taking care of myself inside and out. Becoming desirable has a whole new meaning now. No longer am I looking for acknowledgment from others to feel good enough about myself. I am funny and kind! I am beautiful the way I am! I am desirable to myself!

Loving myself and feeling desirable wasn't the end game. When we open the doorways between our outer-self and inner-self, there is a connection between feeling good emotionally and physically, from which a sense of awakening and living fearlessly transpires. I can finally be myself. I can hear my voice, desires, and purpose on earth. The irrational fear of failure is hushed as I attempt to do what I wouldn't dare to do when I was younger. I started my journey as a stand-up comedian. The liberation and freedom as I spread my wings to test my own limits in life are what I have waited for all my life. I can't believe it took me this long to learn to love, and believe in, myself!

Chapter 15

Rosy

Marley Tufts

"Sometimes the dark things prepare us for the hardest things. I am ready to be that butterfly."

Marley Tufts is a multi-passionate entrepreneur who realized her comfortable, nine-to-five job with benefits wasn't fulfilling anymore. After living through an unexpected and life-altering event, Marley decided to leave her job as a therapeutic recreationist and dive into starting her own business. Taking this leap into entrepreneurship was the best thing she ever did. Marley now empowers others to explore what really lights them up and supports them on their journey as entrepreneurs. Known as the "creative queen" among her friends and family, she loves to explore the ways people can be fun and creative in their business and life. Through coaching, workshops, hard decisions, and adventure, Marley leaves her clients feeling excited and inspired to be their best selves. Marley wants to make the world a better place, and she doesn't care if that sounds corny. She lives to support individuals in realizing their dreams, while also adding her own personal creative touch to everything she does. Marley's life today resembles something she could have only dreamed of during her nine-to-five days. She believes that, in the end, we only regret the chances we don't take.

ig: yourcreativequeen ~ fb: Marley Tufts

t: MarleyTufts

Life as a Caterpillar

I'm a caterpillar that crawls like a worm
Wondering about walking, hoping to learn.
Maybe even becoming a butterfly,
Flying like a bird, touching the sky.
Boom, bang cracks the cocoon.
Out comes something new.
You can see my beauty, but not my cocoon.
Her flying cut through the bumble bee's hive.
Luckily she was okay and she survived.
She lived with the bees and the bugs all very snug.
Sad but true, she died in a hot coffee mug.
- Marley Tufts (age 14)

It was my thirtieth birthday and I was walking down the street, feeling great—on cloud nine!—after a night celebrating with my friends. The sun was shining on my face and the birds seemed like they were chirping a little louder than usual. I had a pep in my step as I headed toward the hospital; I was excited to tell my mom about my fabulous birthday. As I approached the hospital, the place I had visited every day the previous month, my stomach started to turn. I didn't know if it was my hangover kicking in or my gut trying to tell me something.

The sliding doors opened as I walked into the main entrance. Then I headed towards the elevators, passing through the cafeteria. The aroma of the food made me queasy, and I thought I was probably quite hungover. I got in the elevator and my stomach flipped again as I ascended. I heard a ping and looked up as the elevator doors opened to my mom's floor. I was excited to see my mom as it was my actual birthday and she was, quite simply, the birthday queen. I walked into her hospital room with a big birthday grin. She wasn't there. She wasn't there *and* there was a new family taking over the room. My mouth felt dry, my heart sank, and I rushed to the nurse's desk in utter panic.

I knew that after this day my life would not be the same.

"Where is my mom?" I asked the nurse, who appeared to be unnerved by my frantic behavior.

"Your family wasn't updated?" she replied, not realizing that our family wasn't called with a very important update.

She explained that my mom had been rushed to the intensive care unit in the middle of the night because she wasn't breathing.

The rest of my birthday was a complete blur, filled with frustration and fear. I didn't know if my mom was going to make it and I wasn't ready for that. Can you ever be ready for that?

Growing up, my mom, Rosy, was the person I was closest to. She saw me for who I was and loved me unconditionally. I felt like I saw her in this same light: a light of love. She was comfortable in her own skin and I loved that about her. Her contagious laughter could be heard across a room. For her, being a mom was effortless and fun. She always told me and my sister that we were the best things that ever happened to her—she called us her "M&M's"—and we always knew she meant it. Both my mom and dad showed me and my sister how to appreciate the little things in life, like birthdays, cooking, and dancing in the kitchen; we all brought joy to our everyday tasks. When I was fourteen, I wrote a poem called "Life as a Caterpillar" and my mom loved the poem openly and genuinely; it stayed in her mind for years after I wrote it.

"Remember that caterpillar poem?" she'd ask from time to time, and then she'd remind me of how much she adored it.

She always made me feel important. Even when my mom was in the hospital, these qualities continued to shine. She eagerly went on walks outside the hospital to find a patch of sun. She was a ray of sunshine on her ward. The nurses called her "Auntie" and even made her a card for Mother's Day. Her ability to value the little things in life was contagious, and the nurses would even come in on their days off to visit my mom and check in. I continued to be in awe of the impact she had on others.

Days felt like months in the hospital with my mom, especially after she was moved to the intensive care unit. After the fiasco of her being moved so abruptly, my family and I were even more determined to get answers. The medical professionals who examined my mom kept telling us not to worry. "It's not cancer," they said, repeatedly.

Still, we worried; she was sick and suffering. Not knowing what was happening, I took time off work to be with my mom and focus on her. One night, my mom and I were sitting in her room watching *Wheel of Fortune,* one of our many shared favorites. We were chatting through the show, but as it went to commercials, my mom turned to me and said, "I've never seen you so happy."

This caught me off guard as I knew she wasn't talking about the show we were watching. "What are you talking about?" I asked, a little baffled.

"You seem more like yourself lately," my mom continued, "when you're not at work." She spoke simply: "You are different when you're not there."

I realized she was right. As scary and stressful as everything was at that time, I felt a little lighter being away from the job that weighed me down. This job had turned into something that just paid the bills, and the lack of passion I felt for my work was affecting me more than I knew. But my mom saw it. Even as she struggled and suffered, she saw me, and she cared deeply about my happiness. She wanted me, more than anything, to be myself. My mom would never realize that this conversation changed the trajectory of my life.

A few more weeks went by without answers. We spent long days in the hospital, sleeping over, and spending every moment with my mom. Then, on May 6th, 2015, we finally got an answer: inoperable stomach cancer. My world went dark. The pain and devastation are simply indescribable. My dad, sister, and I held on tight to each other knowing we only had months—maybe weeks—left with her. We had to be strong for her, even as we felt our world crumbling beneath us. There were good days, bad days, and all the in-between. We never left mom's side. I realize now how grateful I am for that time: time to laugh together, cry together, and hold on to each moment for what it was; time to have hard and courageous conversations.

Then, my worst fear became my reality. On July 2nd, 2015, I held my mom's hand as she took her last breaths. As much as it's a beautiful thing to be with your loved one as they transition to the other side, it's also the hardest thing, and it leaves an imprint on your mind and soul.

My family and I had to somehow go back to navigating the world without our rock, our favorite person. I didn't know how to do that or what it was going to look like. I kept thinking about the conversation my mom and I had while she was sick. I couldn't get it out of my head. I seemed more like myself when I was away from my job. As time went on, the grief was unbearable, and I thought more about what I wanted in my life. I was sitting in my office one day and thinking of what she said; it was an "aha" moment. I realized I didn't want to spend my life just paying the bills and working a job that didn't bring out the best in me. I didn't want to work to live, I wanted to live and work. I had more to offer. Life is short, what was I waiting for?

As I was navigating these feelings and thinking about what my mom said, the book and movie *Wild* were out and being promoted. *Wild* is a story of a young woman who loses her mom. Watching and reading *Wild*, the main character resonated with me. Like her, I had a choice: after watching the most important person in my life die, I could either go down a dark path, or I could go in another direction. Yes, I could drink, party, and numb out all my feelings. But I knew that wasn't how I ultimately wanted to live my life. I chose a path of light instead of darkness. I was going to make changes in my life and do things that would make my mom proud. So I left the "comfy" job and decided to take a risk: I started my own business. I was grieving the loss of my mom, my everything, and also growing into an entrepreneur. Closing the door on a job that didn't satisfy my need to be creative, grow, and be my best person was the best thing I could have done. It was the light that I needed during the darkest times.

I continue to grow as a businesswoman, learning and experimenting as I come into my own as an entrepreneur. It hasn't been easy. The loving support from my friends and family has helped light the way. Choosing to go for it instead of choosing fear—I dare you to try it! It's the best thing you could ever do, and you can thank me (and Rosy) later.

Even in the darkest moments, it's amazing how we continue to grow. Looking back now, I can't believe I was able to speak at my mom's funeral. I'd always enjoyed public speaking, but to speak at your own mom's funeral? The church was packed and full of love, but I didn't know where to begin. There was so much to say. How could I talk publicly about what I'd lost, about who she was? How could I do this? But I did it. I had written a letter to each of my family members the Christmas before my mom's passing, a letter to express my love for them. I hadn't known it would be the last letter I'd write to my mom.

Dear Mom,

I decided to write you guys a letter. You, Mel, and Dad are the most important people in my life. Yes, it's cheesy, but hey, I thought it was a cool stocking stuffer. Mom, I just wanted to let you know I love that I can call you at any time of day—morning, noon, or night—and we can just chat about everything and nothing. I am so grateful for you always supporting me and cheering me on. You always want the best for me but without the pressure. I especially love when we have our lunch dates or little outings, you somehow always seem to buy me a little surprise or pick something out that I love. We always have so much laughter, and can just go with the flow. I am proud to call you my mom and walk beside you. If I lose you in a store, I can easily find you as I am sure going to hear your laughter sooner or later. You seriously have the best laugh. I love how you are so warm and kind, you will make conversation with people in line at the store. I loved when I lived in Toronto and you were always wanting to give money to the homeless. Dad was like, we would go broke if we lived in Toronto! I especially love how you always say Mel and I were the best thing you ever did. Mel and I are so lucky to call you mom.

Love being your M&Ms. Thanks for always being on my school trips growing up and putting little notes in my lunch box. For cheering me on when I played sports. For loving my poem and always bringing it up as if I have done something so amazing! For always going overboard and packing everything we needed whether it was the beach for the day or a drive. We definitely had snacks and anything we needed. Thanks for always having leftovers for me—frig I love your cooking. Especially love the cheese mash potato pie and of course your meat pies. I remember the one year you made me one for my birthday because I wanted that instead of a cake. Or the time you made one for Martha Stewart and she wrote you a note back saying your pie is better! Do you remember that? So cool!! Speaking of birthdays, thanks for always making every occasion special. Even though I am almost thirty years old, you still have little surprises for Valentine's Day and other occasions, and you make birthdays the best. Remember the birthday we went to see Bob Segar—lol!—we ended up having such a fun, hilarious night. Or the time we went to see Dave Mathews and you liked the opening band better and then halfway through the concert you're like, I thought this was going to be Jack Johnson we were seeing? Anyways, I just wanted to let you know you are such a gift, so lucky that you are my mom and my best friend, not many people can say that. Cheers, mom, to being you, love you so much and look forward to making more memories. Never change.

In case no one has told you, you are awesome and an amazing mom.
Merry Christmas,
Cheers to doing snow angels together!
Love, Mar

***

I was free-spirited and open-minded throughout my life, but even more so after losing my mom. The devastating loss of her taught me that we are truly not guaranteed tomorrow. So now, I embrace my life, my light, and I say yes. Someone asks me if I want to go to New Orleans for a tech conference: Yes! Do I want to go to Ireland? Yes! Am I going on a trip to Boston with my family to create memories? Yes! Going to Florida? Yes! Solo trip to London? Yes! Creating and recreating the life I want? Yes! My mom is on this journey with me and cheering me on every step of the way.

I want people to know, it's not easy, but you have a choice to find the light within the darkness of your experiences and make the most of it. Be extraordinary, be you, and enjoy the little things. It's messy, you will be in the goop, but eventually, you'll be the butterfly.

Chapter 16

My Mediterranean Freedom Trip

Christiane Ghakis

"I don't do guilt anymore—I do freedom!"

Christiane Ghakis is a single mother of two teenagers living in the Montreal area. She graduated as a pharmacist with a master's degree in 2000 and began a career in the pharmaceutical industry. She speaks five languages, due to her Egyptian, Greek, and Italian origins. Never accepting any cultural notions as limiting beliefs and always driven to accomplish more, Christiane completed a doctorate degree in pharmacy in 2018, all while working full time and co-parenting her children. She is currently a leader in a major pharmaceutical firm.

She volunteers as a member of an organization that offers shelter and professional services to victims of family violence, a cause very dear to her heart.

In her free time, she continues to push her limits with scuba diving, kickboxing, and traveling. She can often be found exploring local wrecks or far-off reefs, ideally with her children.

Regardless of her busy schedule, and armed with a special kind of wisdom, she always finds time to offer a compassionate ear to those around her in need.

ig: christiana_.g ~ fb: Christiane Ghakis

li: Christiane Ghakis

Guilt and shame are powerful emotions. Unfortunately, they are sometimes inflicted by those very close to us in order to exercise control or preserve appearances. I first wanted to name this chapter *My Mediterranean Guilt Trip* until I realized that wasn't my story. My story was much more a freedom-finding journey of resilience, the freedom that comes with overcoming limiting beliefs, and letting go of the desire to keep fighting, whether it's for approval or to avoid discomfort. I have often said that "I don't do guilt anymore, I do freedom!" Below is a peek into my journey. I say a peek because there is much more to this story. As I write these words, I hesitate to reveal certain details of the constant fears and stressors I experienced during my younger life. The desire to live free of all these emotions and anchors is what kept me going on this journey to uncovering my inner light.

As a first-generation Canadian woman, born to Christian parents of multiple Mediterranean origins who immigrated to Canada from Egypt, I grew up with two sets of cultural beliefs: those from the Mediterranean culture, interpreted and taught the best way my family and parents knew how; and the Canadian culture and beliefs which were more liberal in the family's eyes. Don't get me wrong, I absolutely love my Mediterranean roots and origins; the beautiful culture, the languages, the music and dancing, how we talk until our hands get tired, and how passionate we are about food! However, as a Canadian-born woman from Montreal, Quebec, I also wanted all the beautiful opportunities this wonderful homeland offered me. After all, I would often hear that our elders immigrated to Canada for a better life!

I grew up experiencing a cultural dichotomy that was often guilt, shame, and conflict-causing. I will elaborate but first, let me explain the family's background. My mother, the seventh of eight children from an Egyptian family, experienced loss and trauma when the family lost their parents early on. Despite my mother losing her mom at the age of four and her father at eleven, she is the kindest and most caring of souls. She was known as the mother in the neighborhood who would take care of and feed everyone, making the tastiest dishes and giving the best advice as a confidant. She gave this love and time to many, despite her own hardships. Needless to say, she was, still is, and always will be my pillar of love, strength, and mostly, resilience.

She met my father, also Egyptian-born but of Greek-Italian origins, upon her arrival in Canada. He was quite the character with little respect for personal boundaries. He spoke and sang out loud, taught us to appreciate food, joked around often—sometimes inappropriately—and also represented a lot that is patriarchal and authoritarian in the culture. This is where the cultural conflict became important and difficult for me as a young woman with aspirations and a desire for independence. I would hear him say encouraging words one moment like "Go to school! Become something! Study hard!" which were all good values that I hear myself repeating to my children. Then, on the contradictory side: "Don't go out! Don't talk to boys! Don't wear black, or lipstick, or nail polish, or a short skirt—you'll look like a . . ." I would very much struggle with these conflicting statements since on one side I was being encouraged to "become" whilst on the other, I felt I was being shamed and made to feel guilty, simply because I was a girl. So, wanting to be the "good girl" and gain paternal acceptance and love, I dutifully did everything I thought I needed to do to be the perfect daughter. I didn't understand until later in life, and after growing through different experiences, that this was the cause of my constant desire for external approval rather than having the confidence within that I eventually acquired.

I knew and felt that my mom loved me unconditionally but with my father, there were conditions that needed to be met, otherwise there would be shame and guilt-inflicting consequences and love withheld. So I became a pharmacist and started my fulfilling career after graduating with a master's degree in 2000. I also completed a doctorate in 2018 while working full-time and raising my children.

This was my secret rebellion. I always knew that because of my academic accomplishments, I would secure a successful career and this success would allow me to be free and never depend on anyone. It was my way out of my stifling and, at times, oppressive childhood. Because of this, I learned to fight to ensure that I would never be put in a situation where I would need to depend on anyone or anything—let alone a patriarchal culture with a belief system that did not hold up in this day, country, and age anymore. This was my rebellion and I pushed through my life accomplishments with this end goal in mind.

I eventually got married, and then proceeded to hear more cultural contradictions and degrading comments once again: "Now you're married and taken care of! I don't need to worry about you anymore!"

I remember thinking: "That is odd . . . I am taking care of myself and my children, making my home and my life . . . Not the other way around!" I did not feel like others were taking care of me and yet was being categorized as such. In fact, as I mimicked my mother's empathy, I would always be the one taking care of others—sometimes forgetting myself in doing so. I also thought this was another interesting dichotomy: to be encouraged to become something but to be dependent on a cultural perception that only allowed you to be fully complete once you had a husband. I didn't think much of it at the time as my desires aligned, however, I always felt I was meant for more and that I had a more progressive mindset.

This would eventually manifest itself when my husband and I separated and I chose self-love and self-preservation. We had purchased our house, had two wonderful children, let life happen to us, and grew apart. I remember feeling like I had "failed at perfection" at the time, but I was also unwilling to sacrifice my future happiness with all the years I had left ahead of me. I felt I had lost so much of it in my childhood that there was no way I would endure losing more moving forward. The mixed feelings that come up when a relationship ends are rarely spoken of in a positive light. His cultural background was very different from mine and I remember thinking to myself on the day we got married how much I loved those differences, as they were so far from the example I had growing up and that this would be good for me. Subconsciously, I believe I chose the complete opposite of what I had as a father figure. It may have been a way to "protect" myself from future anticipated disappointments and limitations and it was also a consequence of the guilt and shaming traumas I had experienced. I likely made a "safe" choice rather than one aligned with my wants and needs. It may have been our differences that made us evolve farther away from each other rather than bring us closer, but I can say today that we were successful in co-parenting and even able to spend quality family time together with the kids on special occasions. I remember thinking as I was about to get divorced that the kids would be okay because we would be careful, or at least try, not to create a difficult ex-spouse situation. I tried very hard to live by this intent despite it not always being easy. What I did not expect, however, was how I would be perceived, by certain family members, once my marriage ended.

Sometimes, the people whom you believe you can count on, are the ones breaking your heart and betraying you. At first, I would pick up on paternal comments such as "Why would you buy a house? We own one already!" The insinuation here was that as a divorcee, I would move back into the family home, a possibility I had never considered. Growing up, I could not wait to get away from everything that was "patriarchal" in my family. It had never served me but rather would cause inner conflicts as I tried so hard to be accepted as the good girl and model child.

Other comments that I internalized as micro-aggressions were: "Why do you need a queen size bed now that you've separated?" Here the insinuation was that since I was alone, a twin bed would do. I actually had a great comeback for that one: "The kids liked to sleep with their mommy!" Here I was, this thirty-six-year-old career-oriented, professionally accomplished, financially independent woman and mother having to justify my furniture choices! I was also adamantly discouraged from purchasing my own home: "What will you do if your roof leaks?" Those were just some of the obvious examples I perceived as degrading.

It all culminated in late 2011 when I was publicly shamed at a family member's wedding, assumingly, because I was getting divorced. I was dancing with family and friends, having the most fun

I'd had in a long time. At that specific moment, I was happy. My six-year-old daughter had fallen asleep on some chairs as we continued to celebrate. At some point, my father decided it was enough and came to tell me, yelling over the music, that I was acting like a ". . ." because I was dancing with other men (there were women too) while my child was sleeping. He physically tried to remove me from the dance floor! I was heartbroken and in shock. I mean, we were dancing, in a circle, to "Living on a Prayer"! I never expected this and would have hoped for a different outcome. Yet, in the face of these betrayals, I decided to remain focused, purchasing my own home as a single mom sharing custody of her five- and two-year-old, while incredulously realizing that "in our culture, it is shameful to leave your husband and get divorced!"

Surprisingly, even some women in my family (and not) perpetuated these behaviors. They would say things like: "She's alone—no one wants her . . . there must be a reason . . ." and "Yes, she's got a degree but she's only smart at school." These comments struck me as odd because I felt they suggested that if you were accomplished professionally, something had to be wrong with you elsewhere. Almost as if professional success prevented a woman from being a good parent or partner.

I've always had the utmost respect for stay-at-home moms—mine was one and she is one of the strongest women I've known. Her strength is based in her compassionate heart because, yes, it does take strength to be compassionate in circumstances when you have all the reasons to be hardened and cold. It seems, however, that some women are taught a misogynistic way of thinking that is perpetuated by the things the matriarchs teach, say, and do. As a female child of this environment, you can choose to conform to and reproduce this because "that's just how things are done" and you are unaware of it. Or, as I did, you can rebel against it because it challenges your core values and you become aware of the limitations it can inflict on you. Not only have I experienced this myself but seen it perpetuated with acquaintances; the fathers, the brothers, and sadly, sometimes, the matriarchs, the sisters, and female in-laws are the reinforcers of this sometimes cultural, shame-based misogyny. It always puzzled me as to how you could inflict this type of stress onto someone close to you in a moment when they are experiencing one of the most difficult choices of their lives and need their support system. Sadly, the expected and hoped-for support system sometimes malfunctions, and that, there, is the heartbreak and betrayal. When this happened to me, I felt hurt and angry. I could not understand the reasons for this since I had tried so hard to be the perfect daughter, mother, professional, and person—I had learned to constantly fight and push through, to "just keep swimming" as the Disney saying goes.

Thankfully, my mother was not judgemental at all. As a child, I had witnessed her strength despite this mentality, when certain members of the family discouraged her from leaving an unsafe marriage while everyone knew exactly what was happening, simply because "there are no divorces in our family." When my marriage was ending and she knew about my efforts to try and make it work, she said to me: "Do what you need to do to be happy. We only live once." She was right.

I realized, because of my two children who absolutely needed the best of their mother, I would put up boundaries and do what I knew best: be resilient once more and fight. This time, however, it was a different kind of fight. I was resisting this acquired belief that I needed to be perfect and "do everything right" (according to who, really?). I was now fighting to take care of us and in order to do so, I needed to let go of this preconceived notion of perfection, or that I had failed and shame would be the consequence. We are all perfectly imperfect and it was liberating to realize I needed to let go of my own anchors to be free. Sometimes, when you feel the need to "just keep swimming" in the face of challenges, you can also decide to stop swimming. Knowing when to do so and learning when to let go of the fear of being shamed is growth. Today, there are moments when these feelings still creep up on me, but as I have said before, "I don't do guilt anymore, I do freedom!" There, too, have been recent moments when I have instinctively wanted to "just keep swimming," but had to catch myself, decide to stop fighting and just let go. The journey is indeed ongoing.

I've always felt the pull to tell my story and believed one day I would write about it. When the opportunity to contribute a chapter to this book was presented to me by a close friend, I knew I had to take it. She suggested that I had a story to tell and that it could help inspire others. I had never thought of it that way, as I felt many have gone through something similar. I decided to step into the unknown and the possibilities this opportunity had to offer. Perhaps this is the first anchor I am releasing in order to eventually uncover more of my light. Maybe, this is yet another meaningful part of the journey on *My Mediterranean Freedom Trip*. Peace, love, and freedom.

Chapter 17

Checkmate

Lisa Howard

"Spirituality is a perspective. Everything is a blessing when you change your perspective."

Since the age of seventeen, Lisa Howard has studied and mastered the art of manifestation. Lisa's dad passed away and she went into the depths of depression, addictions, and anxieties. Growing up in Los Angeles, California—the city filled with not so many Angeles—where people come from all over the world to find fame and fortune, Lisa took a road less traveled. All she wanted was to find true happiness. In her pursuit of happiness, Lisa used astrology, manifestation, and intuition to guide and help her better understand life and the people around her.

Now, after overcoming many obstacles and finding her inner power and light, she helps others do the same. Currently, she is living her favorite manifestation in the beautiful city of Newport Beach, California. Lisa loves murder mysteries, reality shows, and the ocean. Lisa raised two beautiful daughters, Jasmine and Bella, and their family now has a new addition, her grandson.

ig: audaciouslisa ~ fb: Lisa Howard

Hollywood, lights, camera . . . action! My name is Lisa Howard. I was raised in the beautiful paradox of Los Angeles, California. As a child, I was shy and well mannered around most people, but more fun and outgoing around friends I was comfortable with. My dad is a Scorpio, like me. He was super outgoing and fun. As a family, we would have BBQs, go to my grandmother's for holidays and birthdays, and go on vacations. My great uncle was a Green Beret in the Army. The C.I.A. found and hired him in the fifties. My uncle traveled all over the world protecting the Presidents of the United States. Because of his job, he brought my family from New York to Los Angeles. My brother married into the Goossen family, who are well known in boxing. Oscar Dela Hoya fought the Ruelas brothers in my brother's backyard. One of my favorite memories as a child was my aunt taking me shopping at the mall and literally shutting the stores down, buying anything I wanted. I felt like a princess. I was happy.

Raised Catholic, I went to church every week with my grandmother. I even had a nun in my family, Sister Mary Austin, who has now passed on that I still pray to. On the surface, life was great. But behind closed doors, there was abuse. Unfortunately, generational cycles of abuse ran deep in my family.

At the age of nine, my mom had me hospitalized. She claimed I was mentally ill and insisted I was an inpatient client, so I lived at the hospital rather than have outpatient therapy and reside in my family home. A couple of months later, I went back home because it was all insurance would cover. My heart broke as I heard my mom plead to the insurance company to please keep me hospitalized longer. It was no secret I didn't get along with my mom but she was the only one I had issues with. She knew exactly what to say and do to provoke me, then use my reaction to manipulate me out of my home. My mom doesn't have empathy. She doesn't know how to love and doesn't like animals because to love an animal takes that emotional connection she's incapable of. There were days when I would cry and she would just stare at me with no emotion like I was a weirdo. The power a parent has over their child is a power like no other. To not feel loved by a parent, especially a parent of the same gender, is the most painful thing I've ever experienced. As affectionate as I am, anytime my mom got close to me physically, I felt anxious and uncomfortable.

Besides my mom, everyone loved me. I got along with everyone in life and made friends everywhere I went. But at fourteen, my parents lost their rights to me. The courts realized there was more depth to me acting out and took me from my parents rights away. I became a ward of the court. I lived in several group homes and juvenile halls. I made lifelong friends along the way because I knew how to have fun. I had the best sense of humor and I loved pranking the staff and other kids. However, I would cry and wonder why my family never reached out to help me or let me live with them. My aunt told me years later that no one in my family knew my parents ever lost custody of me. My mom would lie and tell people I was at a friend's house or some other excuse.

I was released at seventeen and two months later my dad and grandmother died. I was devastated. Besides friends, they were the only two people I was excited to see when I was released back home. The only two people in this world who I knew loved me.

Though my mom shows many similarities to a narcissist, she hasn't been diagnosed. I was told by many professionals throughout the years, "If you want to be successful in life, stay away from your mother."

They helped me understand what a narcissist is and why it was in my best interest to stay away. I was released to my mother's house at seventeen, right when my dad died. After a couple of months back at my mom's house, I spoke up to my mom because I was being violated by her live-in boyfriend. After years of being pushed to live elsewhere since I was a little child, I was so excited to go home. But my mom told me, "If you don't like it, you can leave."

My mom got jealous when I told her I was violated instead of protective. I moved out. I wish I could say I never looked back. I thought grieving a loved one that passed was the hardest thing I had ever done until I had to grieve the loss of a still-living parent. It was easier to justify by saying, ". . . but it's my mom."

My self-esteem became nonexistent. I had no self-love. Friends my age were too young to understand what I was going through so they just called me weird behind my back and became distant. They didn't understand why I would rather sleep all day than go have fun. After all I had been through, I wasn't able to come home and be that fun, innocent, happy kid anymore, especially after the loss of my dad and grandmother.

Still seventeen, I moved to my boyfriend's house. His family treated me like family. They gave me the kind of medicine we all could use: love. I started my first job at Papa John's Pizza. I loved it! It was exciting. It definitely helped lift my spirits back up. I worked there with my brother and some people we knew from high school. Barnes and Noble, the bookstore, became my favorite place to spend all my extra time. I stayed in the metaphysical section studying astrology and manifestation. I was obsessed. It became my passion. The first book I bought was on how to manifest and I still have it today. My brother's girlfriend at the time pulled up to Papa John's in a new Acura. It was love at first sight. I said to myself, "I want an Acura just like that!" I visualized myself already owning one, did what my manifestation book suggested, and two months later, I owned one.

I had my first daughter at twenty years old. Instead of being excited, the first thing my mom did was call child and family services. She told them I was mentally ill and tried to cause me to lose custody. I never had motherly support or a helping hand. My mom used my daughter as a pawn to hurt me for seventeen years. I even caught my mom messaging a neighbor she knew I didn't get along with to get videos from her front door camera that was faced toward my front door. They would literally watch everything I did, then gaslight me and tell people I was just paranoid. Talk about betrayal. Instead of protecting me, she always has gone with anyone against me to help them hurt me! I had proof of the messages and other situations, yet she would always deny, deny, deny; sing her same song, and say the same phrases she's always said anytime I've tried to hold her accountable. "You don't know what you're talking about,"

"You don't remember it correctly," "You're wrong," "You need medication," and the infamous, "That was in the past, get over it."

My mom was wishing on my downfall, hoping for me to fail. I couldn't ever relax and have fun, or go out with friends for a weekend because my mom was patiently waiting for any reason to get custody of my daughter just to tell everyone, "I told you so."

Suicide was something I attempted a couple of times because to continuously get kicked when your down gets to even the strongest of minds. If you don't have dreams to wake up to, what is there to wake up for? I wasn't born depressed and anxious, quite the opposite, but life is hard enough, especially as a single mom with no family help and a mother sabotaging me. My mother's life depended on me being sick. She never formed her own identity. I became her identity. She financially benefited from my being mentally ill. The first introduction my mother had with anyone—a neighbor, my friends, family, *anyone*—she would tell them I was mentally ill. If a narcissist can't control you, they control how others view you. It was her way to isolate me because, unfortunately, people listened to her side and never got to know me themselves to make their own decision. As soon as anyone labels you, they don't try to get to know you. They judge and stay distant because if my own mother was saying it, it must be true. My mom felt the need to control the narrative. She told everyone that I was mentally ill to hide the fact I was abused and to discredit me to others. She isolated me from my family so I couldn't speak the truth! I walked around life with my head down for so many years. I was tired of people judging me and not trying to get to know me.

It took me thirty-eight years to take my power back! To remember that I am a badass manifestor and I can have any life I want! I finally understood what every professional warned me about my entire life. I was able to take my emotions out and see my mom for who she is. And not just my mom, but anyone with similar traits. Narcissists are everywhere. I learned life was a game to be played. Everything finally just made sense! Dealing with a narcissist is like playing chess, there's no love involved. I sat down and made a plan of what my next chapter was going to be.

Here is my own personal preference as to how I manifest and what steps I take:

First, I set my intentions towards what I wish to accomplish.

I make a vision board that I have posted to see in my room. The key is to not obsess over the vision board but to make it and release it into the universe. Believe it will come and the universe will conspire to make it happen, just let go and have faith. Thoughts are powerful. You have to stay positive.

I water fast. Fasting takes away all of the stuff my body doesn't need and it connects me in a strong way to my higher power.

Be genuine. Karma is real. You can have anything you want in life so watch what you ask for but also, if you're not a good person, you will lose it. The way a person is living is indicative of their karma and their thought process.

I made a vision board. Decided I was going to move to Newport Beach, California to live my dream life. I had the vision and the doors started opening. My oldest daughter turned 18. The toxic dynamic between my mother, daughter, and myself was over. It was then I was finally able to heal. I am still healing as I write this book; it's a process. The more I healed, the more I fell in love with myself. The more I fell in love with myself, the more powerful I became. I got a new car and a new job. My intuition was at its highest. My frequency went up. I started attracting healthy people in my life and I cut off the toxic ones. I was able to let go of addictions. I was so excited to live where I could walk to the beach. I became the healthiest I had ever been physically, mentally, and emotionally.

Now, I ride my bike, play tetherball, and stay active with my daughter. I wake every morning as happy as I did as a kid before anything traumatic happened. I am free. I broke free of an unhealthy family. I'm done being my family's scapegoat! I'm the most confident I've ever been. Adversity builds confidence and mental resilience. Once you have gone to war, you don't come home scared of a fight. I stopped taking people personally who did not understand me and I learned how to accept others for the way they are. We meet people in life where we are at and I'm not speaking physically. I found like-minded people who understood me as I do them. My soul tribe. My chosen family. Teachers are everywhere whether it be learning from a stranger, a neighbor, or through relationships. I learned to look at things from a spiritual perspective. The more I healed myself, the more spiritual I became. I no longer feel alone, even when I am physically alone. I feel my ancestors and higher power every day. Because my faith is so strong, I am able to live free and happy knowing everything will always be ok, not because I moved to the beach and rode my bike. It's not that simple. I put in the hard work to heal myself and transform to be able to ride my bike anywhere I am and feel free and happy.

The older I get, the easier it is to look back and see how everything is connected. For all the good and bad, there is a reason and purpose for everything. We can go through life hating people who hurt us or be grateful for what they taught us. I knew I was healed when I was no longer mad at the pain, people, or problems. I trust my intuition and the universe completely now. I believe rejection is protection and to have been rejected by people along the way is a blessing I am now grateful for.

I decided to write this chapter to inspire and help anyone that has gone through hard times. I love my mom and my family. I am thankful for what they have taught me. Spiritually, I believe I was meant to have my mom to become who I became. For that, I thank her. She taught me how to find genuine happiness within myself; to love unconditionally; to trust my intuition and to stand up for myself; to believe in myself and stay true to my heart no matter how hard anyone tries to gaslight me; and last but not least, to have gained the kind of confidence not many obtain. The type of happiness and confidence I now possess is so far within that no one can break it or take it away. I've earned it. No matter if I have a dollar to my name or not, I know my worth. Life taught me how to be happy with nothing and have the confidence as if I have everything! I wish to bring the topic of narcissism to light because it is so common, yet the abuse is silent. The black sheep are the most woke. It's a blessing to be on the outside looking in because you get the clearest view. Until we heal, the cycle continues. Mother Teresa has a poem I love called "Anyway." The last line in her poem is my favorite. She says, "You see, in the final analysis, it is between you and your God; It was never between you and them anyway."

Chapter 18

Even When The Odds Are Stacked Against You

Rachel Myrick

"Where *is* that line that separates a miracle and a curse? I believe that line, that determining factor, is faith. Faith can turn the darkest circumstances back around. Faith can restore our minds and even our bodies amidst the most unbearable pain."

Rachel is a caring and loving person who strives to help keep those in her shoes alive, even when the odds are stacked against them. Growing up as an only child in Virginia, USA, she is a hands-on creative and a hands-on mother of two with a background in real estate and emergency medicine. Injury and resulting disease ravaged her life when it completely took away her mobility—robbing her of her independence, ability to provide for her family, but most importantly, it took away her ability to parent the way she loves. After more than four years since her injury, Rachel has found a renewed purpose despite her challenging circumstances. Rachel has established a personal following of other pain Warriors who turn to her for advice and direction regardless of their season of life or type of pain. She shares with Warriors from all walks of life how to face the day-to-day struggles of pain vs. self-worth, medication vs. government regulation, navigating physical limitations, maintaining purpose in family life, and tips for facing each new day with renewed hope. Rachel lives one day at a time and reminds everyone facing pain and adversity: We have survived 100% of everything God—and life—has thrown at us so far, and together we can face whatever comes next. You are not alone!

mommaonwheels.com

ig: mommaonwheels ~ fb: Rachel Myrick

li: Rachel Myrick ~ Goodreads: Rachel Myrick

"Whatever you do, *DON'T* Google it. Just get the very first available appointment with this pain management doctor, and do whatever he says. It's going to be a long, hard road ahead. I'm sorry." What in the world had I gotten tangled up in to need that speech from my general practitioner of almost a decade?

I have always been a little clumsy. Over the years, I have dropped and broken the screen on almost every cell phone I have ever owned. So many times, actually, they changed the guidelines on free replacement screens at BestBuy. It might have been partially due to me dropping (and breaking) it in the parking lot on the way to the car after getting it back from the repair department ten minutes prior, but I digress. As a teenager, I would do such silly things that family and friends suggested I be wrapped in bubble wrap to protect me from myself. I was the master of falling *up* the stairs.

Given my history, it came as no shock to my thirteen-year-old son, my boyfriend, and all of his closest friends and family when I dropped my cell phone and wallet on the floor of the restaurant as we were headed through the second door in the portico. Also not surprising to anyone, I too looked as though I was going to tumble onto the floor. What no one knew was that my life was going to drastically change, forever.

Initially, I felt what I believed at the time to be a wasp or hornet-type sting. It was excruciating and caused me to cry out in pain. It was unlike any other sting I had ever felt in my life. As the pain was not subsiding, I dropped (okay, perhaps threw is a more accurate description) my phone and wallet to the ground so I had both hands free to examine my foot for the cause of my pain. When I got down low to get a better look, I felt a second intense pain sensation, this time causing me to reflexively clutch my injured foot. As I was trying to wrap my hands around my foot in hopes of making the pain subside, I felt *it*. It was there—wriggling under the sole of my sandal, startling me and making me flail my foot, shoe, and squirmy foe in an attempt to shake *it* off of me. Cue agonizing pain sensation number three. *It* was stuck to my left foot. Shaking my foot as hard as possible, I screamed out, "I got bit, I got bit!"

I had kicked hard enough this time to finally be free, causing it to fly across and hit the floor in front of my very confused son and boyfriend. A little eight- to ten-inch long, venomous (and apparently hungry) baby copperhead snake.

It bit me three times in total. Once on my middle toe, and twice on the side of my foot just behind the base of my pinky toe; the fang marks remained for months but the effects would last so much longer. The story of a normal thirty-something single mother getting bit by a venomous snake inside of a Longhorn Steakhouse was so shocking that it was trending in the top three news stories on all of Facebook, was also on other social media platforms, and was even gaining the attention of reporters from other countries. It was the snakebite heard around the world. An ambulance ride, a hospital stay, a few vials of antivenin, and a three- to six-month prognosis for getting "back to normal": That should be about where the story ends, right? We all thought that too, but it's the farthest thing from what was ahead for me.

Released home from the hospital after six days, I was non-weight bearing, on crutches, with swelling and discoloration throughout the entirety of my left foot, leg, and up to my hip. Days seemed to drag on. The bruising wasn't resolving and there was an overall dusky purple-gray color setting in. Sleep wasn't coming easily if at all, and the pain was still increasing—each day worse than the one before. That cycle led my primary care physician to refer me to a pain management specialist just two months after my injury. Though my physician of nearly ten years typically had a warm, teddy-bear-like bedside manner, his face alone told me this was going to be quite different. He cautioned me sternly and very matter of fact, "Whatever you do, *DON'T* Google it. Just get the very first available appointment with this pain management doctor, and do whatever he says. It's going to be a long hard road ahead. I'm sorry."

"What is it, doc?"

"I hope he proves me wrong, but I think you have C.R.P.S."

By the time I started at the new doctor, a month had gone by, and in that time things had continued to spiral out of control. I would start to feel similar sensations in my fingertips, then fingers, hands, and arms, all the way into my shoulders. Just as my leg and arms did, a spot on my back the size of a dessert plate would have me writhing in pain if the breeze blew across it. Lord forbid you mistakenly touch a sensitive area, or I would uncontrollably burst into tears. All of his suspicions were confirmed by the pain management doctor as well as second, third, even fourth opinions. It was, indeed, Complex Regional Pain Syndrome (C.R.P.S.) known in the medical field as *the most painful medical diagnosis there is*. Imagine *constant* pain levels topping other painful experiences including kidney stones, unprepared/unmedicated childbirth, and even amputation without medication. This is a reality I will have to live with for the rest of my life. It has since progressed to approximately seventy-five percent of my entire body, even a spot on my face, scalp, and one ear are affected. The progression of the C.R.P.S. in my left leg took less than six months before I needed a wheelchair for mobility. Within one year, I moved into a power chair when I lost most of the use of my arms for prolonged periods of time, leaving me unable to propel the manual wheelchair on my own for more than a few minutes at a time. I was diagnosed with full-body C.R.P.S. which affects an even smaller percentage of people. The spread can continue indefinitely and the sensations and locations increase with age. So, we're in this for the long haul.

What does it feel like? Hell on Earth. Is that an acceptable answer? Well, yes and no. Arguably not the most politically correct answer, but it feels like an incredibly accurate, real, and raw answer. It feels like I am on fire; burning from deep within my bones, radiating out through the muscles and joints, all the way to the surface, coupled with the sensation of a terrible sunburn on the skin level, as though someone is grinding a handful of shards of glass into the already burning skin. Just when I start to question if I can handle another second like this, it doesn't let up; it just up and moves on to other areas of my body. Without warning, without any apparent causation or correlation, it moves. I find I feel much like a rotisserie chicken when trying to lay in my bed and relax. About the time I get my mind around the new location and start to find mild comfort with a particular position and blanket and pillow placement—just as I get as comfortable as the devilish disease will allow—it's off and running to the next location. Destination, unknown.

Modern medicine, in the traditional sense, has no known cure, no FDA-approved courses of treatment, and not one medication specified for use with C.R.P.S. patients. The general treatment pathway is to try medicines developed for so many other conditions, just hoping that if they throw enough things at it, they'll come across the right mix to mediate some symptoms or numb you to the point you no longer feel anything at all. Before being injured, I was only taking a daily multivitamin. Not knowing any better, and blinded by the severity and intensity of the pain throughout my entire body, I was on more than fifteen pills per dose (four doses a day) at one point in my journey. We were trying surgeries as often as every six weeks, for a time. Even after five minor surgeries followed by two overwhelmingly major surgeries into my spinal column to implant electrodes onto the spinal cord itself, this beast still ravages my body. I constantly felt as if I was underwater. As if I could see the light but couldn't get my head to the surface to take a much-needed breath. Ironically, close to half of the medicines I was on were to help with the side effects of the other medicines and procedures they gave me. I felt like a guinea pig, a test subject in my very own medical journey.

The lack of options for my care was maddening. Having no answers and nothing on the horizon to reach for, hope for, or work towards was depressing. This kind of news leaves someone like me, who doesn't take no for an answer, to their own devices. So, I did the only thing I knew how. I Googled it! So very many times since I was first diagnosed, and as recently as just a few days ago, and I will continue to Google it until the results of the search reflect hope, understanding, compassionate care, advocacy, and ultimately a pathway towards pain-free living through remission and/or a cure.

Currently, when you search C.R.P.S., you'll find the stories of doom and gloom, the explicit injury photos that terrify a newly diagnosed person, hopelessness, and then the elephant in the room: the alias. The most prominent and repetitive thing you notice in the search results is the alias; and the single most important reason I fight so hard for my fellow Warriors to feel hope for their future:

Complex Regional Pain Syndrome a.k.a. The Suicide Disease.

The Suicide Disease.

I must have read it a thousand times.

I had to come to terms with the fact that I now have "The Suicide Disease."

While the irony is lost on someone until they know my backstory, it is still a palpable irony that makes the hair on the back of my neck stand at attention, even to this day. Let me explain . . .

Just under a month shy of my tenth birthday, my mom called me downstairs into the living room to sit for a while. I sat with her as she had to explain to my young, innocent self that my grandfather had opted to end his life by his choice and his own hand just one night earlier. Days before my tenth birthday, we would fly out to Colorado to visit with family and console each other. The pain would change over the years, but the experience would begin to shape the rest of my life.

Somehow, this wasn't the only experience I had with suicide. Not even close. On the first day of tenth grade, I learned that a close friend and classmate since kindergarten had opted to end things in his own way as well. In the ten years between ages fifteen and twenty-five, I lost two more family friends; two close personal friends; a coworker; a member of the fire department where I volunteered; a patient I revived in the field who made it just long enough for his family to say goodbye; and multiple patients in the hospital while I was on shift. The total number of successful suicides in my life by the age of twenty-five was fast approaching twelve beautiful souls, combined with countless others who spoke of or attempted self-harm. I was carrying a burden larger than life, and the sheer fact that I now had this disease that drives so many (especially with full-body symptom presentation like my own) to take their own lives to stop this unbearable pain seemed almost like a curse. Almost. However, this isn't horseshoes, and "almost" doesn't count; so where *is* that line that separates a miracle and a curse? I believe that line, that determining factor, is faith. Faith can turn a curse into a miracle. Faith can turn the darkest circumstances back around. It can be the key to uncovering your light even amidst the very darkest of times.

For, at that moment, I realized it was not a question of *why me? Why would He give me this terribly painful disease, and burden to bear?* Instead, led by faith, I knew it was a question of: *How am I so special and so strong that He would trust me with one of His hardest battles?*

I, alone, had seen what suicide does to families, friends, and the survivors left behind. I knew the terrible pain of all of that sorrow; the gut-wrenching screams of a child who lost a parent, and those of a parent who lost a child; the heartbreak of an entire town who lost an Eagle Scout to bullying; and a community who lost a first responder. So many lost souls, all the candlelight vigils, sermons given, prayers said, and the many years of pain and grieving; it wasn't for naught. My old pain had a two-fold purpose: to be a lesson in why not to let the new pain defeat me, and a calling to step up and help others so it wouldn't defeat *anyone else* down the road. I had walked these paths for so long, not understanding why until now.

As I poured over the Google results and the reference information available, I recognized over and over that the search results were going to remain stale, sad, and unchanged if I didn't take matters into my own hands. So that is exactly what I have done. Through outreach in the pain community, speaking to other Warriors, and advocating for all the services we still so desperately need, I am making a change. I am an advocate for equality and for life despite the tough circumstances we face. Each day I am gathering tools and resources to reach people with chronic pain, acute pain, emergent pain, and especially those Warriors with C.R.P.S.

I strive to bring search results for the future that reflect hope, care, love, understanding, pain relief, remission, and cures to all who seek them; enabling all pain patients to take back their power and uncover their own light.

Chapter 19

Choosing Life

Kerri Fargo

"In order to truly heal we need to love and accept all parts of ourselves."

Kerri Fargo is an intuitive healer who sees and feels energy. She has spent the last twenty years guiding others on how to develop their intuition and how to live healthy, joyful, amazing lives.

Passionate about personal growth and spiritual development, she is also trained as a holistic healer, yoga teacher, reiki master, shamanic practitioner, and psychic medium.

She is the founder of Circle of Light® Wellness Centre, Kundalini Reiki® Canada, Soap Planet & Divine Alchemy Bodycare.

When she is not working with clients, you will find her hiking, camping, or bringing groups on spiritual adventures to one of her favorite sacred sites worldwide.

Kerri also enjoys making pottery, jewelry, natural body care products, and (more recently) rescuing and restoring vintage trailers.

A mom to three boys (now amazing young men), she lives in Dundas, Ontario with her magical cat, Merlin.

kerrifargo.com ~ circleoflightwellness.com

ig: reikigirl ~ circleoflightwellness ~ freespiritvintagetrailers

fb: Circle of Light Wellness Centre ~ li: Kerri Fargo

They say confession is good for the soul, so here is mine: I struggled with writing this story.

Believe me, the irony is not lost on me. Here I was writing a chapter in a book about how to shine your light and I was stuck and in fear of shining my own. And this is the problem, isn't it? Somehow, somewhere along the line, maybe in childhood, maybe later, maybe even before birth, we learn that it's safer to stay hidden. If you stay hidden, you can't be seen, and if you can't be seen, then you can't be hurt.

After working as an intuitive healer for the last several years, I can honestly say that this is something we all carry. Whether it's conscious or unconscious, it seems to be a part of being human. Fear is the culprit. It is the number one reason we hold back, and why we hesitate to share the deeper parts of ourselves with others. It causes relationships to fail, bodies to become unwell, and dreams to be lost. It is the destroyer of hope, and I know it well. I have faced it many times, so you would think that by now this would not be an issue for me. But life is like that. It's an evolution, a process of constant growth, and it never stops.

Since childhood, I've perfected the art of staying hidden. As a child I was different. I was overly sensitive; I felt things intensely; I saw things that other people didn't see and heard things that other people didn't hear. I was labeled as shy because my comfort zone was to hold back and energetically read a situation before jumping into it. I felt everything. Other people's moods, thoughts, feelings, and sometimes even their physical pain. As a child, I was taken to the ear doctor numerous times to check my hearing because I wasn't paying attention to the teacher in class. Instead, I was tuning into the energy and spirits around me because I found that much more interesting. I would also have dreams about things before they happened. I remember asking my mom when I was twelve years old if she and my dad were going to get a divorce. She reassured me that was not going to happen, but a year later when they split up. I was devastated. I didn't like being intuitive and I didn't like knowing things before they happened, especially bad things, so I did my best to shut it down and shut it off, and, for the most part, I was successful. But despite my best efforts, my intuition would pop open at different times throughout my life, often during periods of big change or extreme stress. Each time, I would turn it off and tune it out and each time it became harder to do so.

A week after applying to teachers' college, I found out I was pregnant. I had been on the pill but I knew something in my body wasn't right. Sure enough, this baby had magically jumped through the birth control barriers I had in place. The timing was terrible, and I wasn't ready, but I felt in my heart that it was meant to be.

The next year was a whirlwind. Graduating. Moving. Getting married. Having a baby. All wonderful, albeit exhausting, things. I was a stay-at-home mom all day and at night I went back to school. The plan was to become an educational assistant, but a near miscarriage and bedrest threw a wrench in those plans. I was still nursing my firstborn, and I hadn't even had a monthly cycle yet when I found out I was pregnant with twins. It was as though an unseen force kept interrupting my plans. Call it fate or karma, but I was beginning to think I was just meant to have babies. Maybe in a past life I was murdered for not producing heirs because three boys later, the succession to the throne was secure.

My twins came early and soon I was juggling three boys under the age of two. Negotiating colicky premature twins was total insanity, but I embraced being a mother with all of my energy and enthusiasm because I loved it. It grounded me, defined me, and gave me purpose. When my twins were just over a year old, I was finally finding my rhythm and occasionally even getting some sleep! I had just completed a business program and was about to launch my UV protective clothing company. The week before the big launch I was on a much-needed trip with my girlfriends in the Caribbean testing out my samples. While changing clothes I noticed a lump in my breast. I had just weaned my twins so assumed it was from that. After two weeks on antibiotics, the lump had grown from pea-sized to half my breast so my doctor sent me for a mammogram. The mammogram tech refused me because of my young age, and even though I didn't think anything was wrong, something inside of me made me demand to have that test done.

The following week I was in a crumpled heap on my kitchen floor sobbing, thinking I was going to die and leave my children without a mother. I had just hung up the phone on my last chance. The specialist I was trying to get in to see was going out of the country the next day. My life was on the line and I needed this second opinion, but now all hope was gone. Overcome with grief and desperation, I cried for my babies that I would never get to see grow. It was like a surreal dream moments later when the phone rang and the receptionist asked, "Can you get here in an hour?"

That was the first of many miracles that saved my life. A few days earlier I had been diagnosed with aggressive cancer and given a terrible prognosis. It was a complete shock. I thought I was healthy. I took good care of myself. I was training for a marathon. There was no family history and it seemed impossible to be diagnosed with breast cancer at my age.

Thankfully I ended up with one of the best doctors in Canada. When I asked him what my chances of survival were, he handed me an article he wrote with several other doctors about women in my situation. I read it in the car on the way home and by the end of the article, they had all died within a two-year period. I decided right then and there that would not be my fate. I did absolutely everything. Surgery, chemotherapy, radiation, naturopathic medicine, energy work, meditation–you name it; I did it. I'm here today because of my refusal to die, an excellent naturopath, experienced doctors, talented energy workers, and remarkable lines of fate that allowed me to get that second opinion. I'm alive today because I was willing to meditate, excavate, and leave no stone unturned. It was the hardest year of my life, but I managed to get through it.

The soul excavation, the healing sessions, and all of the work I had done resulted in the epiphany that my years of self-rejection and shutting down essential parts of myself had essentially shut down my life-force energy. My body had been running on half power—a weakened battery—for years, and that is what made me sick. That was the moment I realized I needed to love and accept all parts of myself or I would not survive.

That was twenty years ago.

It took my life being on the line in order for me to finally embrace my life. My healing journey was not an easy one. But it made me stronger. It made me fearless. It definitely made me not sweat the small stuff. There is a reason adversity and extreme crisis, or being plummeted into darkness, allow us to find our way, our light, and our essence. It does this by stripping away all the other things in our life that are unimportant distractions until we are left with only ourselves. And it's terrifying, but it is also beautiful and freeing.

There were many things that helped me get through this difficult time. Energy work, meditation, connection to spirit, my energy, intuition, and the soul of who I really was.

Up to that point in my life, I had a plan for my life but it was as though the energy of the universe kept picking me up and moving me elsewhere while I fought it. Throughout my healing process, I finally surrendered and realized I was always being moved to where I was meant to be. Once I stopped spending so much energy denying and fighting who I was, I healed. I surprised my doctors. I surprised myself. I was immensely grateful and every day felt like a miracle.

I threw myself into learning more about these things that had helped me in an effort to understand them better. I had always been aware of my intuition and energy but I didn't have the explanation that went with the experiences. I think that is why I had been so afraid of them. We tend to fear what we don't understand, so I took the time to fill in the gaps in my understanding.

Learning Reiki was a huge turning point for me. This beautiful, gentle, and powerful therapy enabled me to fully open to my intuition in a safe and loving way and allowed me to embrace it. I had learned Reiki to help with my own self-healing, and hadn't planned to use it with others. Coming out the other side of this experience fuelled me with a desire to help others and today I am honored to have worked with so many beautiful souls. I now teach them Reiki as well as how to connect to, develop, and trust their intuition.

Learning to embrace all parts of ourselves is essential. When we deny who we are, it affects our biology and negatively impacts our health. Taking the time to heal and begin the journey back to loving yourself fully and completely is so important.

I did not get through any of this alone. I gratefully accepted help from friends, family, and strangers. I knew this was bigger than me and I needed support.

My boys were the anchor that kept me here. They were still babies. They needed me and I needed to be there for them. This was my desire and focus to keep going. I used visualizations to place myself into the future, to see myself there, to believe it, and to make it a reality. I would meditate and visualize myself a year forward in time, five years, then ten years. I imagined myself at my boys' high school graduation, college graduation, weddings, holding my grandchildren, all of it. I did this every single day.

I made a list of all of the things I wanted to accomplish and experience before I died and attached a timeframe to each of these things. Upon adding everything up I realized I needed to live at least another sixty years. That motivated me.

I used every single resource available to me. Medical and holistic. I did not discriminate. I tried Everything. I am a big believer that we can heal anything with energy and consciousness, but sometimes that can take time. If you need months and an illness is growing in days, then you need more than one thing to tip the scales.

Surrendering and allowing and accepting helped heal my body but it also led me to where I was meant to be. My whole life up to that point had been me trying to get somewhere. Trying to go to teachers college. Trying to start my own business. Trying to be a good mother. Trying to bury my intuition. Trying and pushing takes a lot of energy. And throughout this process, I realized that the part of myself that I had felt was my greatest challenge, that part of me that I tried so desperately to hide, ended up being my greatest gift.

I had to release the parts of myself that didn't fit anymore so that the essence of who I was could rise to the surface. I found courage and strength inside of myself that I never knew I had. I found myself by moving through my darkness. And then years later in the service of others. Today, after working with thousands of clients, I truly believe most illnesses stem from a lack of love. The healing of anything and everything is somehow connected to our love and acceptance and forgiveness of ourselves and others.

In every experience, there is something that we gain, whether it's wisdom, truth, or finding our way. When my doctor gave me two years to live, I was devastated. But it was also a gift. Every moment during and after that has been precious to me. I no longer live my life for other people's agendas. I am free to live. I am free to love. I appreciate life. I don't sweat the small stuff. I never take a single day for granted.

Since then, it's been my mission in life to continually learn, evolve, and face my fears. Every day I endeavor to overcome my limitations, expand my capacity for love and understanding, and upgrade my skills so that I can be a better healer, better intuitive, and a better person on this planet. And I find my joy in helping others do the same.

I believe we are all on a similar journey. Our details are different, but we are all here together. We are all going through variations of this. The separation and isolation I experienced, I never wanted anybody to experience. But the truth is, we must all feel it and face it to become who we are meant to be. We need to be able to go into that fire and know that we will not be destroyed by it, but instead, we will be transformed by it.

We need to overcome our fears. We need to acknowledge our pain and understand our darkness because in doing so we take away the power it has over us. That is how we find our greatest gift. The gift that each of us discovers is how we are meant to show up in the world. It is how we can be of service to help others. By doing so, we can help others find their greatest gift. That is where our path is and that is what feeds our souls. This is what allows us to shine. Not just a little bit but as a bright, brilliant, and blinding light. By overcoming our darkness and disconnection, we can then become the lighthouse for others.

Chapter 20

Only You Can Determine Your Worth

Lisa Pinnock

"Your wisdom, strength, and radiance lie within. There's no need to seek validation of these facts from outside sources. Remind yourself daily of your worth. Be the hero of your own story."

Lisa is an educator, musician, multipreneur, and lifelong learner. She is a bestselling co-author of *Women, Let's Rise*, an award-winning publication by Golden Brick Road Publishing House.

She loves inspiring women to step into their power and light through community building, advocacy work, and healthy eating with Epicure. Lisa leads a local group of heart-centered entrepreneurial women with FemCity, where she is a Global Member and facilitates workshops on their platform. She is very excited about a new venture as a Certified Circle Leader with Woman-Speak, a global organization devoted to unleashing the brilliance of women's voices through unique public speaking practices.

Lisa's involvement as a founding member of Diversity, Equity, and Inclusion Committees with Epicure and FemCity has fueled her mission to highlight and amplify the voices of diverse, marginalized communities. She firmly believes that representation matters, and that our society is strongest when we embrace the full spectrum of humanity.

Lisa brings decades of combined experience and leadership in a myriad of fields, including music education and performance, classroom teaching, liturgical planning, mentorship, and most recently, lead authoring two new book projects with GBR. She is honored to collaborate with the incredible women who have poured their hearts into writing volumes one and two of *Uncover Your Light: Empowering Stories of Hope and Resilience*.

ig: lisampinnock ~ fb: Lisa Pinnock

li: Lisa Pinnock ~ Goodreads: Lisa Pinnock

Mending the Broken Pieces

"All these pieces, broken and scattered; in mercy gathered,
mended and whole.
Empty-handed but not forsaken; I've been set free.
I've been set free."
- Hillsong Worship

The memories of that night are forever etched in my mind. Waking in the middle of the night. The awareness of something not feeling quite right. Stumbling in the dark to find the bathroom. Feeling the urge to relieve myself. Not knowing what would come next. Never expecting that the precious life growing inside me would leave, too. That can't be . . . *how* can that be?! She was just here, a few short minutes ago. Somehow I intuitively discern the gender of our unborn child. But wait . . . what exactly is happening now? My unborn child exits my body, not with the joy that accompanies life, but with the horror of an untimely death. It's happening to someone else, not me. I watch this lady on the bathroom floor, sobbing, frantically trying to explain to her husband what had just occurred. The word "distraught" doesn't do her justice, and consolation is a futile endeavor. How can anyone explain this loss? The truth is you can't . . . you just have to live your way through it.

That was 2001. In the following years, we would welcome with elation two beautiful, healthy babies—Chantelle in 2002 and Mark in 2004. Since those days, I've learned more about how the body internalizes trauma until you take steps to release it. And I've also learned that book knowledge and lived experience can be as unrelated as night and day; they may be linked, but one is not the same as the other. If you live long enough, you discover the pathways toward healing are never linear. They can take you through hills and valleys that would put Mt. Kilimanjaro to shame. But sometimes the deep descents and arduous climbs, what we call "tough experiences," can open us up to the greatness within us. So, Dear Reader, what hidden gems will be revealed through your trials and hardships? Here's a question to answer a question: What's the difference between a lump of coal and a diamond? The answer: a huge amount of pressure. When we frame it this way, we can view our struggles as ways to mend our souls; our challenges are opportunities for expansion and elevation. And those broken pieces? They become our building blocks.

It Only Takes a Spark

A guiding tenet for this compilation was a question I asked myself repeatedly: "How do we shine our light brightly when we've lost touch with who we are?" From the moment I envisioned the book you're reading right now, I felt this point of inquiry deserved exploration, and that looking within would be the only pathway to move us through the darkness.

There are times in our lives—upheaval, loss, pain, disappointment—that come about to crack us open, to lay bare the assumptions we hold about ourselves and others, to bring awareness to the programming and patterns that keep us stuck on a never-ending hamster wheel of our own making. But here's what I've come to learn through some of the darkest moments: They provide opportunities to trust ourselves and the light shining within us, even when that light has been dimmed to a mere flicker. Being a light for others begins with igniting our inner spark. It sounds simple enough, yet it's profoundly challenging when we can't see a clear pathway ahead.

Writing for Healing

There is a story from my childhood that I've heard repeatedly. It details my first foray into the world of published writing. My mom tells it much better than I do, but here's the gist of it: Six-year-old Lisa won a poem-writing contest at her elementary school in Jamaica (Immaculate girls, represent!) and as a result, the piece was included in a local magazine. As far back as I can remember, my parents always made a point of celebrating our achievements, big or small. I'm certain my brother, Roger, would back me up on this.

When I reflect on these practices now, I realize my mom and dad were sowing seeds of confidence, self-esteem, and a joy that comes from within. I hope I possess the character to plant the same seeds in my precious children.

From my elementary school beginnings in Jamaica to high school and beyond in Canada, I leaned toward subjects such as English and creative writing that valued writing as a skill to harness rather than a by-product to learn something else. A child's spark grew into a flame.

My brother, Roger, backed up by the oratory skills honed through his law profession, took on most of our family's verbal acts of expression, the family speeches. And in the Pinnock household, there were opportunities galore for those! Where I shone was in creating moments of communication in ordinary interactions—thank you notes, pen pals near and far (especially my cousins Nicky and Michelle in Jamaica), and emails to customer service departments, the good and not-so-good kind. No format was too mundane. It was worthy as long as it was sincere, thoughtful, and created a connection with the person on the receiving end. My sense of growth and joy from writing continued to flourish, and it was bliss. Those life experiences, from a six-year-old poet to an adult scribe, prepared me—and not by accident, I might add—for this very moment: Connecting with you, my Dear Reader, to share stories of hope and resilience by inspiring women from all walks of life.

Recently, I came across a gratitude journal from the start of 2019. It wasn't unusual for me to keep volumes like these over the years, but this particular time frame was significant as it marked the end of a twenty-year marriage. Reading my words from 2019, I saw a map of my emotions, complete with signposts to navigate, and ultimately, a tool to heal and grow. I didn't make the connection at the time, but those entries served a greater purpose than recording thoughts on a page. They offered safe passage through an undercurrent of swirling emotions; the things that were omnipresent but mostly hidden from the light of day. Without the time machine of my journal, my memory—fallible because I'm human—would look back simplistically and only register a heavy blanket of despair with no rhyme or reason. My journal became a place to understand—a tool to manage my upheaval in the present moment of writing and future moments of reflection.

In April 2021, I made a journal entry to my unborn child:

Dearest Emma, Although I never got the chance to meet you, I felt you growing inside me for several weeks. It was a beautiful time in my life that I'll always treasure. When I felt you leave my body, there was so much grief and heartache, and I've been carrying around that pain for far too long. I received your message today through Lorree that it's time to let go. Your soul is safe and happy and that's such a relief. God bless you, my first little angel. Mama will always love you.

I couldn't imagine a better example of how the healing properties of writing offered me respite and comfort during trying times. My trusted journal acted as a time machine once again, allowing me to revisit a pivotal moment that shaped me; it served as a torch to light the terrain of my understanding of what I was experiencing in those difficult periods. I realize now that without it, I would be left fumbling in the darkness of my erroneous recollections.

I bring up these particular examples because they are archetypes of the most valuable lesson I can teach anyone about writing. It is more than record-keeping and even more than connecting with others. It is about nurturing the most important relationship you will ever have: the relationship with yourself. The act of giving your voice a place to speak gives it credence. You validate the person you are and the emotional currency you hold at that moment. When nobody is around and you have no one to please, you get to find out who you really are. Write down those discoveries, and jump into the time machine of your journal when it suits you, to shine a light on those reflections.

The good news is there's no correct way of writing for yourself. Use a pen. A keyboard. Even a voice recorder. Make your sentences short. Make them long. Or don't use sentences—use keywords. Record events. Ask questions. Journaling doesn't have to be lengthy or perfect. Leave the social conditioning of judgment behind; nobody will grade you on your journal. Just make it easy to become a habit; for example, keep your journal nearby and avoid setting rules such as length of entries. After a while, you'll soon discover your voice flowing onto the page if you haven't already. But don't trust me. Trust yourself. Start writing.

Self-Worth Is An Inside Job

"Self-worth comes from one thing—thinking that you are worthy."
- Wayne Dyer

We've all heard the saying, "Happiness is an inside job." I'd take it a step further to assert that the starting place for one's happiness is knowing your worth and seeing your value—not through the eyes of others but through your own. For many years, I held the misguided notion that my value was intrinsically tied to the activities I did, and how well I executed them. Every perceived failure to meet these societal (and self-imposed) markers created another crack in the mirror in which I viewed myself. And it didn't need to be huge incidents to cause these fissures. Forgot a form for the kid's school trip? *Clink*. Didn't remember to grab a key ingredient for dinner? *Crunch*. Call it people-pleasing tendencies, call it perfectionism . . . It was all an unhealthy recipe for self-blame and shame. I see now that these practices readily gave away my power because, on some level, I felt undeserving of determining my own worth. American author and keynote speaker Tim Fargo was spot-on with this quote: "If you want to improve your self-worth, stop giving other people the calculator." Word.

So let's consider some ways to fortify our sense of self-worth. I feel it all begins by first cultivating an unwavering belief in yourself—that you are enough. Period. No apologies or qualifiers. This revelation didn't occur to me until recently, so I'd love to save you, Dear Reader, from the heartache of not-enoughness. Here's what I've found to be true in my journey so far: When we believe in ourselves, trust our inner guidance, and love ourselves unconditionally, we create containers of safety where our superpowers can be revealed to shine brightly. It *all* starts with us.

My first co-authored book, *Women, Let's Rise*, was published by Golden Brick Road Publishing House in October 2020. That experience opened up a whole new set of opportunities, including the book you're holding right now! For that, I'm eternally grateful. In my chapter entitled "Trusting Your Intuition," I shared a checklist of ways to tap into your intuitive powers on a daily basis. The following is a compilation of actionable steps I've incorporated since that time. Some are my tips, others are ones I've gleaned from working with incredibly talented people along the way. My hope is that they'll serve you in the process of uncovering your radiant light. Trust me, it's there, and the world needs it now more than ever.

We have the capacity to know instinctively which direction to turn in times of need. *Practice trusting yourself by attuning to the frequency of your inner voice daily.*

We can lean on each other in times of adversity or struggle. When we harness our collective energy with positive intentions, we all win. *Practice building meaningful connections with people who uplift, challenge, and motivate you.*

Take time to check your "internal battery" several times a day (thank you, Jennifer Lyall). Ask yourself: How am I doing mentally, physically, emotionally, and spiritually? *Practice getting in touch with your needs in the present moment.*

We are all made up of energy, and we often take on both the positive and negative vibrations of those around us without even realizing it (thank you, Sara McCready). *Practice good "energetic hygiene" by grounding and clearing your environment daily.*

Speak life-affirming, loving, positive words to yourself as often as possible. The ability to create the self-image of your dreams lies in your hands and yours alone (thank you, Karen Fiorini and Sandy Rutherford). *Practice loving yourself, first and foremost. It will pay huge dividends.*

We have a choice in how we view any situation. Are you willing to open up to a shift in perspective? To see that life is happening *for* you, not *to* you? *Practice reframing disempowering stories as they arise to ones that serve you.*

We need to feel all aspects of what we're going through—the good, the bad, and the ugly. Skipping this step only delays the emotional recovery and healing that awaits on the other side of our pain. *Practice surrendering and trusting that the process is for your highest and best outcomes.*

The revelations I've experienced and shared here didn't occur in a vacuum, but by intentionally exploring my inner landscape.

Such an excavation tends to uncover things you've kept hidden for ages—things that require the light of day to heal and transform. When we commit to fully embracing the space of growing into our higher selves, we signal to the Universe that we're ready for the abundant blessings that await us.

My deepest desire for you, Dear Reader, is that you'll reflect on your pathways toward healing through the stories within these pages. For me, an incredible dream has already manifested because you are holding this book. And my wish is you'll take away exactly what you need to truly see yourself and to become the light that's always been inside you.

Acknowledgments

I want to thank my family and friends who supported me throughout my career. I would be nothing without you. To my dad: you were brilliant with words; I dedicate this to you.

– Andrea Beneteau

Much appreciation to our friends and family, Summit Church, our counselor Carrie, our kids, who grew alongside us, Lisa Pinnock, who encouraged me to share my story, and God, who is always faithful.

– Stéphanie Rourke Jackson

To my Mom, Dad, Arlene, and Ed: We did it! Immeasurable endless gratitude and thanks to the village that raised me and for those who continue to do so now. I am truly blessed.

– Denise Ledi

I dedicate this chapter to my father, James Carlin. May your memory continue to inspire through the words that I have woven onto these pages. Until we meet again . . .

– Siobhan Carlin

Special thanks to Lisa Pinnock, for her vision for *Uncover Your Light, Volume 2*, to my fellow authors, who are the bravest, most resilient, loving souls I have ever met, and to all those at Golden Brick Road Publishing who worked so hard to ensure this book is available for the readers who need it the most.

– Rebecca Russell

I would like to thank my sons for keeping me inspired to be and do better. I want to shout out to my sister friends who are always there to support me. I am truly blessed.

– Sylvia Calleri

Thank you to my family, especially my husband Craig Phair who puts up with all of my crazy. He is my biggest supporter and fan. To all my clients and the Healthy Happy Whole community for being my readers/editors. And to Lisa Pinnock for introducing this opportunity to me. I will be forever grateful.

– Molly Phair-FNTP, CPT

Thank you Mom and Dad for never giving up on me, even when you didn't understand. Thank you Sandy Rutherford for helping me believe in myself again!

– Sonya van Stee

Thanks to those who showed me the way, whether through adversity or leadership. You were part of my journey. Special thanks to my children who I learn from every day.

– Helen Harwood Snell

Thank you to my incredible husband, my loving parents, my family-in-law and friends, and all those who helped me rediscover my light. I am forever grateful.

– Laura Dawson-McCormack

To Luke for being my catalyst for change, to Valerie and Sean H. for being my biggest cheerleaders, to Maria for being my "crazy doctor", and to my parents and siblings for your love and support. Special thanks to Louisa, who brought me onto this amazing journey.

– Christina Tam

Thank you, Lisa. Without a chance meeting in a random networking event, this wouldn't have happened. To Sasha, for being one of the best human beings on the planet. Carly, Anita, and Oliver, for being the rocks in our lives. Westin, thank you for building this amazing life we have and continuously working to obtain our vision.

– Sandra Blais

So grateful for my life partner's support, my daughter who shows me how to dream and be a better person, my sisters and mom for having my back, the rest of my circle who always uplifts me, and to Lisa and GBR for giving me this opportunity.

– Rupinder Sidhu

Immense love to Daniel, Elliot and Renee, J.R, and E.R who continue to teach me to be a better human being and fill my heart with joy and love. To my cousins and girlfriends. Thank you for being my light!

– Eva Wong

Thank you to my mom, who showed me so much about life. Thank you to my dad and sister, who are always there for me, always cheering me on. Huge shoutout to my friends, family, and community for their love and support.

– Marley Tufts

Thank you Nada, for seeing my light and connecting me to this project. Mom, for your everlasting love. My children: "ALs" for being my light. My friends: Caroline, Leonie, Tamara, Luc, and Greg who were my pillars of strength in recent years.

– Christiane Ghakis

To all my weirdos, outcasts, underdogs, misfits, and the misunderstood, this is for you. Keep being you and you will find your tribe in life. Don't change for anyone. I love you! Thank you.

– Lisa Marie Howard

Mike, for your unwavering love and support and for carrying me all of the times I couldn't walk this path on my own, I love you and can never thank you enough! To my Mom and Dad, and my children—Makenzie, Dylan, Alex, & Cameron—thank you for always being by my side and helping me through each season of this craziness. I love you all.

– Rachel Myrick

To my incredible family and friends for your love and support. To my mom who always goes above and beyond. To my boys Hayden, Logan, and Noah for making me a mom and bringing so much joy to my life. To my guides and angels for always being there. To my clients and students who inspire me daily. And to Ky-Lee and the GBR team for sharing these stories with the world.

– Kerri Fargo

To my Mom and Dad who nurtured my love of writing from a young age. To my family and friends who've encouraged me in all facets of expression. To H.H. for the editing support. To my inspiring co-creators in my book adventures: Thank you for your trust in me, in the process, and mostly, in yourselves.

– Lisa Pinnock

Link arms with us as we pave new paths to a better and more expansive world.

Golden Brick Road Publishing House (GBRPH) is an independently initiated boutique press created to provide social-innovation entrepreneurs, experts, and leaders a space in which they can develop their writing skills and content to reach existing audiences as well as new readers.

Serving an ambitious catalogue of books by individual authors, GBRPH also boasts a unique co-author program that capitalizes on the concept of "many hands make light work." GBRPH works with our authors as partners. Thanks to the value, originality, and fresh ideas we provide our readers, GBRPH books are now available in bookstores across North America and have won multiple awards.

We aim to develop content that drives positive social change while empowering and educating our members to help them strengthen themselves and the services they provide to their clients.

Iconoclastic, ambitious, and set to enable social innovation, GBRPH is helping our writers/partners make cultural change one book at a time.